BEGINNER'S ITALIAN

BEGINNER'S ITALIAN

JOSEPH F. PRIVITERA

HIPPOCRENE BOOKS
New York

DEDICATION

In 1943, during World War II, I was asked by St. Louis University to devise and direct an Italian language program in the Army Specialized Training Program. The goal was to teach about one hundred GI's to speak Italian fluently within the period of a year. These were the young men who were designated to help rule Italy during the Occupation at war's end.

With the help of half a dozen colleagues, we put the lads through a rigorous training program which forbade the use of English from day one. They attended class eight hours a day, five days a week. Anyone caught speaking any language other than Italian was denied weekend leave.

It was a tough drill, but at the end of the year, each and every soldier was speaking Italian as fluently as any educated Italian.

It is with fond recollection, that I now dedicate this simple Italian grammar to the memory of those stalwart young men.

TABLE OF CONTENTS

GRAMMAR LESSONS

INTRODUCTION

It is said that Italy gave civilization to the world. A slight exaggeration, perhaps, for with the combined culture of ancient Rome, Italy has indeed given a large measure of civilization and culture to the world. Take this simple fact, for example. Catherine de' Medici (1519-1589), daughter of Lorenzo II, married the Duke of Orléans in 1533. Before leaving for France, she had a large crate packed with silver plate and cutlery, to accompany her on her trip, for she had learned that, even at the royal court, the French had not as yet learned to use forks, knives, and spoons. Catherine later became Queen of France, when her husband succeeded to the throne as King Henry II.

Note, too, that Tuscany alone has more classified historical monuments than any country in the world. The traveler to Italy will be regaled by the world's finest art and thousands of Roman and Greek monuments scattered from north to south. Little wonder then that Italy has become one of the world's most favored vacation lands.

Italians are gentle, passionate, and family oriented. Their food is simple and delicious, close to the nature that supplies it. Bite into a peach from any region and you will enjoy a fruit that is more fragrant and delectable than any manufactured dessert. The country's beverages are made from the fruit of the land and are mostly non-alcoholic, though Italians drink wine with their meals. Their pre-prandial drink is usually a bittersweet, reinforced wine like vermouth or Campari.

They are a musical people who adore opera and the many bands that give concerts in the town square during festivals and on Sundays. Rare is the family that does not have one or two accomplished musicians. It is a country rich in art, music, and literature.

There are still spoken some 450 principal dialects, derived from Latin. Most Italians speak both their hometown dialect and Italian, one of the most beautiful languages in the world.

We trust that this modest volume will serve as a basic guide to Italy's land and people. The Italian lessons are simple and easy to learn and will help the tourist better understand one of the most interesting and amiable people of the western world.

GEOGRAPHY

Italians call their peninsula *Lo Stivale,* the boot, for the shape it resembles, as it plunges down from mainland France, Switzerland and Austria, into the waters of the Tyrrhenian, the Adriatic and the Ionian Seas.

The country is divided into twenty regions, which in turn are divided into provinces. These regions, in large measure, reflect historical divisions and are colored by different local customs and dialects. One can tell the difference between a Neapolitan speaking Italian and a Venetian. Each region and, for that matter, many provinces, are distinguished by a local accent in their Italian, correct and grammatical though it may be.

The North is divided from the South, not only in speech, but in economic development: it is one of the most advanced industrial societies in the world. The South, on the other hand, which begins somewhere between Rome and Naples, is agricultural and not as well developed. More than any other part of Italy, the South has suffered repeated invasions by foreigners, absolutist regimes, and historical neglect. But despite these adversities, it is one of the most beautiful parts of Italy.

Piedmont and **Lombardy,** the northwest regions, make up the richest and most cosmopolitan part of the country. Turin and Milan, their capitals, are Italy's wealthiest cities. In the north the Alps invite hiking and skiing, while the lakes and mountains of Lombardy are tourist attractions. To the south, the small region of **Liguria** is known as the Italian Riviera. Its capital, Genoa, has been a major maritime center from the Middle Ages to the present.

The tiny region of **Valle d'Aosta** has some of the most frequented ski resorts and is bordered by the tallest of the Alps, the Matterhorn and Mont Blanc. To the east, **Trentino-Alto Adige** marks the beginning of the Dolomite mountain range and is home to Italy's largest national park, the Stelvio.

The Dolomites move on to the northeastern regions of the **Veneto** and **Friuli-Venezia Giulia**. Venice, of course, is the city of principal interest in this area and not far from the watered city lie the historic cities of Verona, Padua and Vicenza. To the south, the region of **Emilia-Romagna** has enjoyed Italy's postwar industrial boom and has a standard of living on a par with that of Piedmont and Lombardy. Politically, it has been a stronghold of the Italian left.

Central Italy is perhaps the best-known part of the country. **Tuscany**, with its rolling hills and the art centers of Florence, Pisa, and Siena, is one of the most visited regions. Nearby **Umbria** has become an increasingly busier tourist center, as visitors are drawn to such cities as Perugia, Spoleto, and Assisi. To the east is **Marche**, which may soon become equally attractive to tourists, its highlights being the ancient towns of Urbino and Ascoli Piceno. To the south are the twin regions of **Abruzzo** and **Molise**, whose hills rise into mountains, with the Gran Sasso, the country's highest peak. **Lazio**, to the west, though generally poor, has Rome as its principal city, once the capital of the Roman Empire and now the country's capital. As a tourist attraction, it surpasses every other part of Italy.

The South really begins south of Rome, with the region of **Campania**, whose capital, Naples, once the capital of the Spanish Bourbon Kingdom of the Two Sicilies, is the spiritual heart of the Italian South, with some of Italy's most interesting ancient sites in Pompeii and Herculaneum, in addition to the country's most spectacular stretch of coast around Amalfi. **Basilicata** and **Calabria**, which make up the boot's toe, have no art centers, but do have beautiful landscape and unspoiled coastline. To the east, at the heel of the boot, **Puglia** boasts thriving, active cities in Bari, its capital, and Lecce, both of which have first-rate universities. One tourist attraction here is the landscape of the Gargano peninsula, famous for having attracted Normans to the area in the ninth century. Puglia also has much neglected Norman architecture, with homes and public buildings built by the Normans or by their descendants. To the south lies the island of **Sicily**, the birthplace and home of

Archimedes, with more ancient Greek ruins than are to be found in all of Greece. Tourists are especially drawn there by a couple of Italy's fanciest beach resorts, in Taormina and Cefalù. But above all, the tourist will find in Sicily a land apart from and quite different than the rest of Italy. Its climate, for one, is the mildest in all of Italy, which speaks of its closeness to Africa, a mere hundred miles to the south. The island was occupied for centuries by the Greeks, the Romans, the Arabs, the Normans, the French, and the Spanish, all of whom have left their mark on the landscape, the people and the language. **Sardinia**, too, feels far removed from the Italian mainland, especially in its undiscovered interior. Its beautiful beaches have recently begun to attract Italians from the north and Europeans.

CLIMATE

Italy's climate is the most inviting in Europe, with warm, dry summers and mild winters. There are regional variations with the more temperate climate in the north and the Mediterranean warmth of the south. *Ferragosto* (august, the holiday month) is what the Italians call the months of July and August, when they themselves go on vacation. The weather can be very hot during that period and the cities overcrowded. It is best to avoid traveling to Italy during *Ferragosto*. For the best weather and smaller crowds, the best times to visit Italy are from April to late June, or September and October.

HISTORY

Italy's history as a nation begins in 1860, when Giuseppe Garibaldi and a small group of ragamuffin soldiers routed the Bourbon army of 15,000 from Sicily and the lower boot and freed southern Italy from Spanish domination. He turned over the reconquered land to the Piedmontese, who then set up an Italian nation under the King of Sardinia.

That is Italy's political beginning, but its true beginning goes back to the year 476, which marks the end of the Roman Empire. That was the year when Romulus, the last of the Roman rulers, was deposed by a barbarian general.

From that year until 1860, the peninsula, Sicily, and Sardinia were subjected to the greedy control of foreign powers and locally entrenched feudal lords — Franks, Lombards, Arabs, Normans, French, Spaniards, Catalonians, Napoleon, Austrians, and the Papacy, to mention the principal marauders; there was a host of other foreign powers, too many to record here. An Italian child studying his country's history can never memorize the thousands of political and military moves that shifted back and forth from the Alps to the waters of the Mediterranean.

Freed from most foreign domination in 1860, the rest of its history boils down to an attempt on the part of patriots and rogues to forge a republic; but this did not occur until the twentieth century. Even then, there was an interregnum in the democratic process when Benito Mussolini seized power and ran the country under a brutal dictatorship.

Now, free at last, Italy is a vibrant democracy with a healthy economy and an important role in the European community. And yet, as though preordained by some superior being, the South still needs attention to eradicate large belts of poverty. However, tourism, which has become quite active there, may bring economic prosperity. Increasingly, northern Italians, Europeans, and Americans are finding a haven in the gentle climate and hospitable people of the South. As tourism grows, more roads, hotels and restaurants will be built, especially in the remote areas of Calabria, Basilicata, and Sicily. (The important town of San Fratello, for example, does not have a single restaurant or hotel!)

ECONOMY

There are two economies in Italy: that of the North and that of the South. The North has cities with skyscrapers and industry, equal to that of any European or American city. The South still suffers from neglect and has a much lower living standard than its northern compatriot. The contrast is such that a Northern League has been formed in the north, with the goal of separating from the South, which it considers a burden to its economy. The League would like to divide the country into its two economic levels, the rich and the poor. If it one day gains political power, we will again see a divided Italy.

The prosperous North contains 59 percent of Italy's land and 63 percent of its population. Of the country's ten major cities, only Naples and Palermo are in the South. The economic flourishing is centered in three northern cities: Turin, Italy's Detroit; Genoa, a major shipping center; and commercial and industrial Milan.

Along with the booming automobile industry, other important engineer-driven industries manufacture electrical supplies, agricultural machinery, ships, and airplanes. Other dominant sectors are textile and chemical manufacturing, ceramic and glass production, and food processing — especially pasta and tomato paste for export.

The success of these enterprises must be credited in great part to an amazing number of native industrial geniuses. First among them was Giovanni Agnelli, co-founder of the Fiat auto company in 1899. Not far behind were Camillo and Adriano Olivetti, a father and son who manufactured typewriter and business machines. Another industrial giant was Enrico Piaggio, who converted his family's bomb-wrecked airplane factories to the production of Vespa motor scooters. It is said that Italy may not invent all of the new industrial products, but it can and does improve any product it produces to a stellar rank, such as the Alfa Romeo and Ferrari luxury cars.

Lombardy, with Milan as its capital, is not only the country's industrial center but also the heart of Italy's best farming region. Only 23 percent of Italy's lands are both flat and fertile, and most of this favorable terrain lies along the Po River in Lombardy, Emilia-Romagna, and Venetia. The North grows a variety of crops, including wheat, rice, corn, oats, sugar beets and vegetables. Cotton and flax grow in the Po Delta and cattle are raised throughout the valley.

CINEMA

What characterizes Italian filmmaking is its move out of the studio and into the country's actual towns and landscape. This was an innovation with which the rest of the cinematic world has not yet fully caught up. A quick listing of some of the major producers and films will tell the reader to what extent this has become the hallmark of the Italian cinema. All are groundbreaking masterpieces of the art.

- **Luchino Visconti:** *Obsession*, an adaptation of *The Postman Always Rings Twice*. A film version of Lampedusa's masterpiece, *The Leopard*.

- **Roberto Rosselini:** *Rome, Open City*. A film version of Giovanni Verga's novel, *The House by the Medlar Tree*.

- **Vittorio De Sica:** *Bicycle Thieves.*

- **Federico Fellini:** *La Dolce Vita.*

- **Pier Paolo Pasolini:** box office hit, *Decameron*, based on Boccaccio's fourteenth century tales.

- **Michelangelo Antonioni:** *L'Avventura*, which uses Sicily's volcanic landscape as a backdrop.

- **Francesco Rosi:** *Christ Stopped at Eboli*, based on Carlo Levi's masterpiece by that name. The filming of a complete opera, *Carmen*.

- **Giuseppe Tornatore:** Oscar-winning *Cinema Paradiso.*

• **Michael Radford:** *Il Postino.*

• **Roberto Benigni:** Oscar-winning *Life is Beautiful.*

Naples and Sicily have become the most vibrant sectors of the Italian film industry. Note that at the 1998 Venice Film Festival there were no fewer than fifteen new Italian films compared with twenty from the United States — an impressive undertaking.

ARTS AND LETTERS

Architecture, sculpture, painting, music, and letters; the list of Italy's accomplishments in these creative arts is breathtaking. All we can do in this brief introduction is give a passing glance at some of the highlights. The reader can regale himself by visiting museums, which exhibit the endless parade of Italian art, and by reading the many good translations of Italian poetry, novels, and nonfiction.

ARTS

Italy's artistic history begins with the **Etruscans**, whose culture spanned from the seventh to the first centuries B.C. Museums in Florence and Rome display some of the few extant examples of beautiful Etruscan sculpture. Surprisingly, some wall paintings have survived and may be seen at Paestum, Tarquinia, and Chiusi. All display bold drawing, bright colors, and lively details.

Both the Etruscans and the Romans were indebted to the Greeks for their art forms. Some of the more famous pieces of Roman sculpture, for example the *Apollo Belvedere* and the *Venus of Cnidos* in the Vatican, and the *Medici Venus* in the Uffizi, are actually copies of lost Greek originals. The Empire's contribution to artistry is exemplified by Rome's portraiture, usually characterized by a bony facial structure, bare forehead, and large eyes. Though many marble busts have survived, the bronze equestrian statues were later melted down, with the exception of the statue of Marcus Aurelius in Rome. Wall painting was also prevalent, the best examples of which are to be found in the towns of Pompeii and Herculaneum. These were preserved when they were buried in the ash from the eruption of Mount Vesuvius in 79 A.D.

Italy's age of artistic leadership began in the thirteenth century when a simple Tuscan shepherd boy, Giotto di Bondone (1266?-1337), looking with wonder at the natural world, painted what he actually perceived. With this simple act he became, along with his friend Dante, one of the founders of the Italian Renaissance. By drawing and painting with a new kind of naturalness, Giotto launched a revolution. He replaced the stiff and gloomy traditional images with live people and some elements of real landscapes, soft luminous coloring and feeling for three-dimensional forms. Legion are the names of painters who followed. We name but a few of these Renaissance artists: Fra Angelico, Filippo Lippi, and Lorenzo Ghiberti who spent almost fifty years sculpting scenes from the Bible on two pairs of doors. One of his pupils, Donatello, soon excelled the master. With his *David*, Donatello reintroduced the nude statue to art.

In 1469, twenty-year old Lorenzo de' Medici came to power in Florence and soon brought under his patronage every talented painter and sculptor. It was under his wing that the Renaissance developed into the greatest period of art in world history. In painting, the roll call is seemingly endless: Andrea del Verocchio, Domenico Ghirlandaio, Sandro Botticelli, Andrea del Sarto, Raphael, Michelangelo, Antonello da Messina, Coreggio, Tintoretto, Veronese, Leonardo da Vinci, Tiepolo, Canaletto, and Chirico, among many others.

In sculpture and architecture, Ghiberti and Donatello were followed by Della Robbia, a terra-cotta sculptor, Verrocchio, Bramante, Michelangelo, Palladio, Bernini, Ponti, and Manzù.

The list of musical composers is not as extensive, but each of these composers is responsible for innovations that changed the course of world music, from the sixteenth century on:

• **Palestrina**: liturgical music.

• **Jacopo Peri**: operas, *Dafne, Euridice.*

• **Claudio Monteverdi**: madrigals, operas, *Orpheus* and *The Coronation of Poppea.*

- **Arcangelo Corelli**: instrumental music, violin sonatas, concerti grossi.

- **Alessandro Scarlatti**: operas, cantatas.

- **Antonio Vivaldi**: concerti grossi, *The Four Seasons*, operas, nonextant; influenced Bach.

- **Giovanni Battista Pergolesi**: opera, *La serva padrona*, chamber cantata, *Orpheus*, church music, *Stabat Mater*.

- **Luigi Boccherini**: chamber music, pioneer in history of stringed-instrument music.

- **Luigi Cherubini**: operas, *Medea*, church music.

- **Niccolò Paganini**: violin music, concertos and capricccios.

- **Gioacchino Rossini**: operas, *L'Italiana in Algeri*, *The Barber of Seville*, *William Tell*, etc.

- **Gaetano Donizetti**: operas, *Lucia di Lammermoor*, *Don Pasquale*, *The Daughter of the Regiment*, and *La Favorita*.

- **Vincenzo Bellini**: operas, *Il Pirata*, *La Sonnambula*, *Norma*, *I Puritani*.

- **Giuseppe Verdi**: operas, *Nabucco*, *Ernani*, *Macbeth*, *La Traviata*, *Rigoletto*, *Il Trovatore*, *Un Ballo in Maschera*, *La Forza del Destino*, *Don Carlos*, *Aida*, *Otello*, *Falstaff*, and the Manzoni *Requiem*.

- **Ruggiero Leoncavallo**: *I Pagliacci*.

- **Giacomo Puccini**: operas, *Manon Lescaut*, *La Bohème*, *Tosca*, *Turandot*, *Madama Butterfly*.

- **Piero Mascagni**: *Cavalleria Rusticana*.

- **Gian Francesco Malpiero**: operas, ballets, choral works, string quartet and symphonic music.

- **Ottorino Respighi**: operas and instrumental music, *The Fountains of Rome*, *The Pines of Rome*, *Feste Romane*.

- **Luigi Dallapiccola**: twelve-tone music, settings of Greek lyrics, operas, *Volo di Notte*, *Il Prigioniero*, and *Job*.

LETTERS

Italian was formed as a language by the year 900. In the Middle Ages, it was the universal practice for the literate to use Latin as their medium, as the nascent language was not considered sufficiently dignified for the writing of prose and poetry.

Dante (1265-1321) wrote fluently in Latin, but he felt that it was proper to use the vernacular to write poetry. He did so in two of the most beautiful works of poetry in Italian history, *Vita Nova* and the *Divine Comedy.* But he wrote in Italian apologetically, and feeling the need to justify his initiative, actually wrote an apologia in Latin.

During his late years, Dante was joined in the literature of the Italian language by the great lyric poet, Petrarch (1304-1374), and his love poems, *Il Canzionere;* and, contemporaneously, by Giovanni Boccaccio (1313-1375), author of *The Decameron.* These works played no small part in establishing the Italian language as an accepted literary medium. With each successive century, a number of first-rate writers contributed to form the cadre of one of the world's great literatures. Again, we may name but a few of the most outstanding:

- **Niccolò Machiavelli**: *The Prince.*

- **Lodovico Ariosto**: poetry, *Orlando Furioso.*

- **Francesco Guicciardini**: History of Florence and of Italy.

- **Pietro Aretino**: dramatist and satirist.

- **Benvenuto Cellini**: autobiography, *The Life of Benvenuto Cellini.*

- **Torquato Tasso**: poetry, *Aminta* and *Jerusalem Delivered.*

- **Giovanni Battista Vico**: philosophy, *On the One Principle* and *Principles of a New Science.*

- **Carlo Goldoni**: dramas, *La Locandiera, Women's Gossip,* and *The Tyrants.*

- **Vittorio Alfieri:** poetry and dramas, *Maria Stuart, Myrrha,* and *Saul.*
- **Alessandro Manzone:** novelist, *I Promessi Sposi* (The Betrothed).
- **Giacomo Leopardi:** poetry, *Song of Italy.*
- **Giosuè Carducci:** poetry, *Hymn to Satan, Barbarian Odes, Rhymes and Rhythms.*
- **Giovanni Verga:** among the top two or three novelists, *The House by the Medlar Tree* and *Cavalleria Rusticana.*
- **Italo Svevo:** novelist, *Confessions of Zeno.*
- **Gabriele D'Annunzio:** poetry and novels.
- **Benedetto Croce:** philosophy and criticism, *The Philosophy of the Spirit, History as the Story of Liberty.*
- **Luigi Pirandello:** Nobel Laureate in Literature, dominated the stage in the twentieth century, *Six Characters in Search of an Author, As You Desire Me.*
- **Grazia Deledda:** Nobel Laureate in Literature, novelist, *Elias Portolu, The Faults of Others, The Mother.*
- **Giuseppe Tomasi di Lampedusa:** *The Leopard,* thought to be the finest Italian novel.
- **Giuseppe Ungaretti:** poet, *Joy, Grief, The Feeling of Time,* and *Life of a Man.*
- **Ugo Betti:** dramatist, *Goat Island* and *The Gambler.*
- **Eugenio Montale:** poet, Nobel Laureate in Literature, *Finisterre, Cuttlefish Bones, Le Occasioni.*
- **Ignazio Silone:** novelist, *Fontamara, Bread and Wine.*
- **Salvatore Quasimodo:** Nobel Laureate in Literature, poetry, and classical translations.
- **Carlo Levi:** narrative of social conditions, *Christ Stopped at Eboli* and *Words are Stones.*

- **Alberto Moravia**: novelist, *The Women of Rome, Bitter Honeymoon*, and *Two Adolescents.*

- **Cesare Pavese**: novelist, *The Moon and the Bonfires, Before the Cock Crows,* and *The Burning Brand.*

- **Elio Vittorini**: novelist, *In Sicily* and *The Red Carnation.*

- **Natalia Ginzburg**: novelist, *A Light for Fools* and *Voices in the Evening.*

- **Italo Calvino**: fables and novels, *The Baron in the Trees* and *Italian Fables.*

- **Leonardo Sciascia**: novelist.

PRACTICAL ADVICE FOR EVERYDAY LIFE

GETTING THERE

1. By Air

Alitalia, Italy's national airline, has the most varied routes between the
United States and Italy. There are daily flights to Milan and Rome
from New York, Boston, Miami, Chicago and Los Angeles. The American airlines fly to Milan and Rome from fewer American cities: *Delta
Airlines* flies daily from New York non-stop, or from Chicago and Los
Angeles with stopovers in either New York or a European city; *TWA*
flies daily from Los Angeles and Chicago, via New York; *American Airlines* flies directly to Milan only from Miami and Chicago. If you wish
to make a European stopover, you have the choice of the following airlines with service to Rome and Milan: *British Airways* (via London);
Air France (via Paris); *Lufthansa* (via Frankfurt or Munich); *Iberia* (via
Madrid); *Sabena* (via Brussels); *Swissair* (via Zurich); *Icelandair* (via
Luxembourg); *KLM* (via Amsterdam) and *SAS* (via Copenhagen).
These airlines have service to Rome and Milan.

Direct flights take nine hours from New York or Boston, twelve hours
from Chicago, and fifteen hours from Los Angeles. Add between an
hour and fifteen minutes to three hours more for connecting flights
to Sicily.

Round-trip fares to Rome or Milan vary little between the airlines. From
New York or Boston, the cheapest round-trip fare starts at approximately
$650 during the off-peak season (November to March); rises to $750
during the shoulder seasons (September-October and April-May); and
peaks at $950 during the summer months. Add about $200 to these
fares if flying from Los Angeles, and $100 if flying out of Miami or
Chicago. Add-on fares from Milan or Rome to Palermo or Catania
range from $100-200, depending on the season and the airline.

2. Through Packaged Tours

The following agencies offer group travel and tours in Italy:

Adventure Center (1-800-227-8747)
   Offers a hiking tour, starting at $800, not including airfare.
American Express Vacations (1-800-241-1700)
   Individual and escorted tours throughout Italy.
Archaeological Tours (212-986-3054)
   Escorted archaeological tours, from 14 to 17 days, around $4,000.
CIT Tours (212-697-2100)
   Escorted tours.
Globus-Cosmos (1-800-221-0090)
   Escorted and individual tours of Italy; prices start at $1300.
Italiatour (1-800-237-0517)
   In conjunction with *Alitalia*, offers fly-drive tours and escorted and
   individual tours.
Mountain Travel-Sobek (1-800-227-2384)
   Offers a "Sicilian Adventure," a hike to the summit of Mt. Etna and
   a visit to the Aeolian islands, for around $2250, excluding airfare.

GETTING AROUND

1. By Train

The trains are operated by the *Ferrovie dello Stato (FS)*, the Italian State
Railways. For the most part, trains do leave on time.

There are seven types of trains:

Pendolino, first-class intercity service on whose ticket includes a seat
reservation, newspapers, and a meal.

Eurocity trains connect the major Italian cities with centers such as
Paris, Vienna, Hamburg and Barcelona.

Intercity trains link the major Italian centers. Reservations are obligatory and a supplement of about 30 percent of the ordinary fare is added. If the supplement is not paid before getting on board, a much bigger surcharge will have to be paid to the conductor.

Diretto, Espresso and *Interregionale* trains are the common long-distance expresses, calling only at larger stations. The *Regionale* services stop at every place no matter what the population. Smoking is not allowed on these lines. Tickets must be validated (punched in a machine on the station) an hour before boarding. It pays to have a seat reservation *(prenotazione)* on the main routes. Note the following signs displayed on the boards at the station:

Partenze, Departures
Arrivi, Arrivals
In Ritardo, Delayed

The price of tickets is reasonable as they are charged by the kilometer. A single second-class, one-way trip from Milan to Bari, one of the longest trips you are likely to take, currently costs about L80,000 ($50) by *Intercity.* Sleepers are available on many long distance services. Expect to pay an extra L30,000 ($20) or so for a couchette, and a lot more (about L75,000, $45) for a place in a sleeping compartment.

2. By Bus

Buses are usually quicker and more reliable than trains. Regional buses *(autobus* or *pullman)* travel to almost anywhere you want to go. City buses are quite cheap, charging a flat fare of 800-1300 Lire (50-75 cents). Bus terminals are scattered all over town, though buses usually pull up in one particular plaza.

There is no national bus company. These are the major Italian bus companies:

Autostradale, Piazzale Castello 1, Milan (tel. 02 801 161)
    Services Lombardy, Liguria and the Lakes.

Lazzi, Via Mercadente 2, Florence (tel. 055 363 041)
    Services around the country.
Sita, Viale dei Cadorna, Florence (tel. 055 483 651)
    Services most parts of Italy.

3. By Air

ATI, the domestic arm of Alitalia, operates flights throughout Italy. This is the most expensive form of travel and should be used only when you are in a hurry to cover long distances. For example, a one-way fare from Venice-Rome is around L225,000 (about $140), and a Milan-Naples flight costs around L295,000 ($185).

4. By Car

Car rental in Italy is expensive: approximately $320 per week for a small hatchback with unlimited mileage. The major chains have offices in every larger city and at airports, train stations, and city centers.

Car Rental Agencies in the U.S.

Auto Europe: 1-800-223-5555
Avis: 1-800-331-1084
Budget: 1-800-527-0700
Dollar: 1-800-421-6868
Europe by Car: 1-800-223-1516
Hertz: 1-800-654-3001

ACCOMMODATIONS

Accommodations are strictly regulated and are fairly reliable. Hotels are rated and must post their prices clearly in each room. It is advisable to establish the full price of your room before accepting it. Booking ahead is recommended especially during July or August, and booking ahead is mandatory for Venice, Rome and Florence from Easter until September.

Prices vary from the poor South to the prosperous North, so the following costs per night are estimates:

One-star hotels charge L60,000 ($40) for a double room without a private bathroom; L60,000-90,000 for private facilities, and not much under L90,000 ($55) in Florence, Venice, Milan and Rome, even without private bath.

Two-star hotels generally cost up to L120,000 ($75) for a double with private facilities, as well as TV and telephone.

Three-star hotels charge a minimum of L120,000 for a double with all the above amenities and, in some cases, a swimming pool.

Four-star hotels cost a minimum of L200,000 ($125).

Five-star hotels have no limit on cost.

Many hotels automatically add the price of breakfast to your bill, whether or not you take it. Breakfast at a local bar is considerably cheaper (and tastier).

MONEY

The lira is Italy's common currency. The exchange will vary, up or down, at around L1,675 to the dollar. Traveler's checks and credit cards are accepted at all hotels in the larger centers. Traveler's checks can be exchanged for liras at any bank.

FOOD AND DRINK

Like most Italians, you may want to start your day in a bar. Their breakfast consists of a coffee with hot milk (*cappuccino*) and a *cornetto*, a jam, custard, or chocolate-filled croissant. Breakfast in a hotel is unappealing, more expensive, and to be avoided.

Sandwiches (*panini*) are usually quite substantial and can satisfy your luncheon needs at a cost of about L3,000-5,000 ($2-3).

Pizzerias are everywhere as well as the **tavola calda**, a sort of stand-up snack bar. The **rosticceria**, whose specialty is spit-roasted chicken, offers another alternative.

RESTAURANTS

Full meals can be taken at *trattorias* or *ristoranti*. The first option is cheaper and features home style cooking. Restaurants are more upscale, with tablecloths and waiters. A meal (*pranzo*, lunch, *cena*, dinner) starts with an antipasto. A plateful of cold dishes costs around L10,000 (under $7). A full meal starts with *il primo*, soup or pasta, for L6,000-12,000 ($3.50-7) and goes on to *il secondo*, the meat or fish dish, for L12,000-18,000 ($7-11). Side dishes (*i contorni*) are ordered separately. Ask for the bill (*il conto*) at the end of the meal. It will include a cover charge (*bread and cover*), around L1,500-3,000 per person, and service (*servizio*), another 10 percent (though it can go as high as 15 or even 20 percent). You won't be expected to tip if service is included; otherwise, leave a 10 percent tip (not expected at pizzerias and trattorias).

BEVERAGES

Italians are not hard drinkers. They drink wine from childhood, but only as part of the main evening meal, or, on Sundays and holidays, at midday. Families that have access to a country place, or who live in the country, make enough wine in the fall to last them throughout the year. For those who wish to quench their thirst with soft drinks, Italy offers a host of delicious concoctions made from a wide selection of fresh fruit. One can also order a *spremuta*, a fresh fruit — orange, lemon, or grapefruit — squeezed on order at the bar.

Walking down the street by a bar in the main square, one would think it was Brazil, from the strong fragrance of coffee. Italian coffee is usually the strong *espresso*, or the *cappuccino* or *caffelatte*, *espresso* mixed with warm milk. Then there is the *frullato*, a fresh shake made with several fruits, as well as the *granita*, a crushed ice-drink, made with coffee or a variety of fruit juices. *Acqua minerale*, mineral water, is always offered in restaurants, as an alternative to wine or to mix with it.

POST OFFICE, TELEPHONES AND MEDIA

The post office is open Monday through Saturday from 8:20 A.M. to 6:30 P.M. It closes at noon on the last day of the month. Stamps can be bought in *tabacchi* (tobacco shops), and at the post office. The *tabacchi,* as well as bars and some newsstands, also sell *gettoni* (L200), tokens for use in telephones, though these are being gradually phased out. *Schede telefoniche*, telephone cards, are available for 5,000, 10,000, and 20,000 liras from *tabacchi* and newsstands.

The best way to make international calls is to use the card issued free by AT&T Direct Service. The company's international operator will connect you and add the charge to your bill back home. International calls can also be made from booths that accept credit cards. Collect calls can be made by calling AT&T's international operator, who will connect you at no charge.

In addition to the national newspapers, *La Republica, Il Corriere della Sera* and *L'Unità*, one can purchase any number of local regional papers. For sports fans there is the *Gazzetta dello Sport*. English-language newspapers are also available in the large centers.

There are three state-run TV channels, *RAI, 1, 2* and *3*, which have less advertising than the independent channels owned by Berlusconi, who has served as Prime Minister. *RAI*'s radio stations were more professional than those run independently. But once Berlusconi came into power, he installed his own men in the *RAI* stations, converting them to sycophantic outlets like those of his Fininvest network.

FESTIVALS

There are colorful festivals throughout the land during *Carnevale* (Carnival or Mardi Gras), the five days before Lent, sometime between the end of February and the beginning of March. Easter Week is a period of great festivity with processions and dramatic events. The biggest celebration is at *ferragosto,* the Feast of the Assumption on August 15, when spectacular fireworks are held.

Every town has its own local saint, whose statue is paraded through the streets amid prayer and frivolity. These processions are very colorful and carefree, reminding one of Carnival.

LANGUAGE LESSONS

THE ITALIAN ALPHABET

The Italian alphabet consists of the following twenty-one letters:

a (ah) b (bee) c (chee) d (dee) e (eh) f (EH feh) g (gee)
h (AH kah) i (ee) l (EH leh) m (EH meh) n (EH neh)
o (aw) p (pee) q (koo) r (EH reh) s (EH seh) t (tee)
u (ooh) v (vee) z (ZEH tuh)

PRONUNCIATION

Italian spelling (orthography) is fundamentally phonetic: **mamma** (Mah mah*), mama,* **pane** *(*PAH neh), *bread.* The stress falls on the next to the last syllable (penult): **p<u>a</u>rlo,** *I speak.* Otherwise, stress is indicated in this text by a bold, italicized vowel: **p***a***rlano,** *they speak.*

VOWELS

a, like *a* in 'father': as in **p<u>a</u>dre,** *father,* **m<u>a</u>dre,** *mother.*

e, like *e* in 'best': as in **b<u>e</u>lla,** *beautiful.*

i, like *ea* in 'beast': as in **f<u>i</u>glia,** *daughter.*

o, like *aw* in 'claw': as in **l<u>o</u>,** *the.*

u, almost like *o* in English 'to': as in **t<u>u</u>tto,** *all,* **<u>u</u>no,** *one.*

CONSONANTS

b, f, l, m, n, p, q, t, v are pronounced as in English. Two consonants are written with two letters (digraphs), **ch** and **gh**.

c, before *e* or *i,* sounds like *ch* in 'choose,' as in **dolce,** *sweet;* it is like the English *k* before *a, o, u:* as in **<u>c</u>asa,** *house.* It also has the *k* sound when it appears as **ch** before *e* or *i* as in **chi,** *what.*

d, like *d* in English **do,** as in **<u>d</u>anno,** *harm.*

g, before *e* or *i,* sounds like *g* in 'George,' **gelo,** *frost* and **già,** *already.* It has the sound of *g* in 'gone' before *a, o, u:* as in **gatto,** *cat,* **gola,** *throat.* The digraph **gh** has the same hard sound before *e* or *i:* as in **ghiaccio,** *ice.*

h is always silent: as in **h**anno, *they have.*

i, unaccented, before a vowel, is pronounced like English *y:* as in a**i**uto (ah YOU too), *help;* p**i**ù (pYOU), *more.*

n, before a **q**, a hard **c** (before **a, o, u**) or **g** sounds like English *ng* (*wing*): as in ba**n**co (BAHNG-koh), *bench;* lu**n**go (LOONG-go), *long* and ci**n**quanta (ching-KWANTA), *fifty.*

r, when single, is formed with a quick flip of the tongue on the palate behind the front teeth: as in ca**r**o, *dear;* pu**r**o, *pure.* When **r** is double, or when it is the first letter in a word, the tongue is suspended between the roof and the bottom of the mouth, not touching either; its sides are curved against the sides of the mouth, while the tip is rounded to let the air escape as in **r**uota, *wheel;* ca**rr**o, *cart.*

s is pronounced like English *s* in 'soon,' but with a much sharper sound: as in **s**olo, *alone;* **s**pina, *thorn.*

s before a sonant (**b, d, g, l, m, n, r, v**) sounds like the English *z;* as in **s**birro, *cop;* **s**degno, *scorn;* **s**granare, *to shell;* **s**litta, *sleigh;* **s**malto, *enamel;* **s**nello, *slender;* **s**radicare, *to uproot;* **s**velto, *quick, alert.* Otherwise, s and double s are pronounced like English *s* in 'see': as in que**s**to, *this.*

u, unaccented, before a vowel, sounds like English *w:* as in q**u**ando (KWAHN-doh), *when;* q**u**attro (KWAH-troh), *four.*

z and zz are generally pronounced like a long and vigorous *ts:* as in **z**io, *uncle,* pre**zz**o, *price.* In the following words, however, z and zz are pronounced like a prolonged **dz;** a**zz**urro, *blue,* me**zz**o, *half.*

Note these combinations:

gl, when followed by a vowel, has an *l + y* sound: as in a**gl**io (AHL yoh), *garlic;* fi**gl**ia, (FEEL-yah), *daughter.* The *g* is not sounded.

gn is like the *ni* in 'onion' as in **ogni**, *every*. The *g* is not sounded.

qu is always like *kw*: as in **quattro** (KWAT-troh), *four*; **quindici** (KWIN-dee-chee), *fifteen*.

sc before **e** and **i** is nearly like *sh* in 'ship'; as in **sciallo** (SHALL-loh), *shawl*; **scemo** (SHEH-moh), *silly*.

In double consonants, both letters must be sounded, the first at the end of the preceding, the second at the beginning of the following syllable: **anno** (AHN noh), *year*; **quello** (KWELL loh), *that*.

m, n and r, when preceded by an accented vowel and followed by another consonant, are prolonged: **sempre** (SEMM preh), *always*; **tanto** (TAHNN toh), *so much*; **parte** (PAHRR teh), *part*.

Italian words are divided in such a way that, if possible, every syllable shall begin with a consonant: **quan-do**, *half*; **no-ta**, *note*; **nor-te**, *north*.

The consonant clusters **st**, **tr**, **gn**, and **gli** belong to the syllable that follows: **fe-sta**, **o-gni**, **al-tro**, **a-glio**.

ABBREVIATIONS

adj.	adjective	indef. art.	indefinite article
adv.	adverb	inter.	interjection
adv. phr.	adverbial phrase	m.	masculine
cond.	conditional	n.	noun
conj.	conjunction	past. part.	past participle
d.o.	direct object	pl.	plural
def. art.	definite article	prep.	preposition
f.	feminine	pres. part.	present participle
fut.	future	pret.	preterite
i.o.	indirect object	pron.	pronoun
imp.	imperative	s.	singular
impf.	imperfect	vb.	verb (infinitive)

ITALIAN WORDS AND PHRASES IN COMMON USE

buon giorno	*good morning*
buona sera	*good afternoon — evening*
ciao	*hello — good-bye*
arrivederci	*good-bye*
per favore	*please*
grazie	*thanks*
mille grazie	*many thanks*
prego (I beg you)	*you're welcome*
come sta?	*how are you?*
bene	*well — I'm fine*
scusi	*excuse me*
mi dispiace	*I'm sorry*
signor	*mr.*
signora	*mrs.*
signorina	*miss*

LEZIONE PRIMA

LESSON ONE

AL AEROPORTO

Marco e Maria Martini arrivano a Roma da Nuova York.

Marco: Maria, sai che il nome di questo aeroporto è Leonardo
            da Vinci, ma tutti lo chiamano Fiumicino.

Maria: Lo so... Guarda, adesso bisogna presentare i passaporti.

Marco: Il Consolato Italiano a Nuova York mi disse che non
            bisogna più vidimare il passaporto.

*Marco porge i passaporti al ufficiale per farli stampare. Nella dogana c'è
una linea per i turisti che hanno qualche cosa a dichiarare e un' altra per
quelli che non hanno niente a dichiarare.*

Marco: *Al ufficiale.* Non abbiamo niente a dichiarare.

L'Ufficiale: Potete passare.

Marco: Scusi, ma dove possiamo prendere un tassì?

L'Ufficiale: All'uscita a destra.

Marco: Grazie. Andiamo, Maria.

Maria: Hai prenotato una camera per due al albergo?

Marco: Ma certo. *Al autista di tassì.* Al Albergo di Roma, per
            favore.

L'Autista: Si Signore.

AT THE AIRPORT

Mark and Mary Martin arrive in Rome from New York.

Mark: Mary, you know, don't you, that this airport is called the Leonardo da Vinci, but that everyone calls it Fiumicino.

Mary: I know, but look, we have to present our passports.

Mark: I was told by the Italian Consulate in New York that it is no longer necessary to have a visa.

Mark hands their passports to the officer to have them stamped. At Customs there is a line for tourists who have something to declare, and another for those who have nothing to declare.

Mark: *To the Officer.* We have nothing to declare.

The Officer: You may pass.

Mark: Excuse me, but where can we get a cab?

The Officer: At the exit on the right.

Mark: Thank you. Let's go, Mary.

Mary: Have you reserved a room for two at the hotel?

Mark: I have. *To the taxi driver.* To the Roma Hotel, please.

The Driver: Yes sir.

VOCABULARY

a	in, to
abbiamo	we have
adesso	now
aeroporto	airport
al	to the
albergo	hotel
altra, un'altra	other, another
andiamo	we go, let us go
arrivano	they arrive
arrivata	arrival
autista di tassì	taxi driver
bisogna	it is necessary to
camera	room
c'è	there is
che	that
chiamano	they call
Consolato Italiano	Italian Consulate
cosa	thing
da	from
destra	right (side)
di	of
dichiarare	to declare
disse	told, said
dogana	customs
dove	where
due	two
e	and
è	is
farli	to have them
grazie	thanks
guarda	look
hai	you have

hanno	they have
i, *m., pl.*	the
il, *m., s.*	the
in	in
lezione	lesson
linea	line
lo	it
ma	but
ma certo	of course
nella, *f.*	in the
niente	nothing
nome	name
non	not
Nuova York	New York
passaporto, -i	passport, -s
passare	pass
per	for, to, in order to
per favore	please
più	more, anymore
porge	he hands over, gives
possiamo	we can
potete	you may, can
prendere	to get, to take
prenotato	reserved
presentare	to present
prima	first
qualche	something
quelli	those, the ones who
questo	this, this one
sai	you know
scusi	excuse me
si signore	yes sir
so	I know
stampare	to stamp
tassì	taxi

turista, -i	tourist, -s
tutti	everyone
ufficiale	officer
una, *f.*	a, one
uscita	exit
vidimare	to certify

LOCUZIONI — EXPRESSIONS

chiamano questo aeroporto Fiumicino	they call this airport Fiumicino
guarda	look
bisogna presentare i passaporti	we have to present our passports
non abbiamo niente a dichiarare	we have nothing to declare
potete passare	you may pass
dove possiamo prendere un tassì?	where can we get a cab?
all'uscita a destra	at the exit on the right
andiamo, Maria	let's go, Maria
hai prenotato una camera?	have you reserved a room?
ma certo	of course, I have
per favore	please

ESERCIZI — EXERCISES:

1. Copy the text, read it aloud and translate it.

2. Translate into Italian:
   Where can we get a cab?
   Everyone calls this airport Fiumicino.
   Did you reserve a room for two?

3. Translate into English:
   Adesso bisogna presentare i passaporti.
   Potete passare.
   nella dogana
   l'ufficiale

4. Memorize the following:

non abbiamo niente a dichiarare	we have nothing to declare
all'uscita a destra	at the exit on the right
guarda	look
potete passare	you may pass

GRAMMAR

I. ARTICLES

The article agrees with its noun in gender and number.

A. *The Definite Article*

Masculine

Singular, **il**   Plural, **i**

il padre, *the father*   **i** padri, *the fathers*
il figlio, *the son*   **i** figli, *the sons*

Feminine

Singular, **la**   Plural, **le**

la donna, *the woman*   **le** donne, *the women*
la madre, *the mother*   **le** madri, *the mothers*

Before a vowel:

Masculine

l'   **gli**
l'occhio, *the eye*   **gli** occhi, *the eyes*
l'angelo, *the angel*   **gli** angeli, *the angels*

Feminine

l'   **le**
l'ora   **le** ore

B. *The Indefinite Article*

Masculine

(a) **Un** before a vowel or any consonant except **s** + consonant, or **z**.

un anello, *a ring*   **un** padre, *a father*

(b) **Uno** before **s** + consonant, or **z**.

uno specchio, *a mirror*   **uno** zio, *an uncle*

Feminine

Una   **Un'** before a vowel.

una madre, *a mother*   **un'**ora, *an hour*

The indefinite article is omitted in Italian before a predicate noun (a noun used with the verb *to be*), expressing occupation, condition, rank, or nationality, but not modified by an adjective.

È poeta, *he is a poet.*   Sono italiani, *they are Italians.*
È medico, *he is a doctor.*

But it is used when the noun is modified by an adjective:

È **un** buon medico, *he is a good doctor.*

ESERCIZI — EXERCISES:

Translate the following into Italian:

1. Mark Martin is a doctor.

2. Mary Martin is a professor of English.

3. Gianni is a good poet.

4. The mother is Italian.

LEZIONE SECONDA

—◆—

LESSON TWO

LE PRESENTAZIONI

Due coppie si conoscono nel aeroplano. Marco e Maria Martini, Gianni e Anna Orlando.

Marco: Permettetemi di presentarmi. Mi chiamo Marco Martini e questa è mia sposa, Maria.

Gianni: Piacere di conoscervi. Io mi chiamo Gianni Orlando e questa è mia sposa Anna. Parlate italiano così bene che forse siete nati in Italia.

Marco: Il fatto è che siamo nati in America, figli d'Italiani.

Maria: E abbiamo sempre parlato italiano in casa.

Anna: Vuole dire che avete sempre parlato italiano e inglese.

Marco: È proprio così. E voi, siete Italiani?

Gianni: Sì, ma abbiamo visitato alcuni parenti in America e ora stiamo ritornando a Milano, la nostra città, dove siamo tutti e due professori di francese. E voi che siete?

Marco: Io sono medico, e mia moglie è professore d' inglese.

Gianni: Sentite, ecco il mio numero di telefono. Se potete visitare Milano, chiamatemi e venite passare uno o due giorni con noi.

Marco: Con piacere. Mille grazie.

INTRODUCTIONS

Two couples meet on the plane. Marco and Maria Martini, Gianni and Anna Orlando.

Mark: Allow me to introduce myself. I am Mark Martini and this is my wife, Maria.

Gianni: Glad to meet you. I am Gianni Orlando and this is my wife, Anna. You speak Italian so well that you must be Italian.

Mark: The fact is we were born in America of Italian parents.

Mary: And we have always spoken Italian at home.

Anna: That means you have always spoken Italian and English.

Mark: That's right. Are you Italians?

Gianni: Yes, but we have been visiting some relatives in the States, and we are now returning home to Milan, where we both teach French. And what is your profession?

Marco: I'm a doctor and my wife teaches English.

Gianni: Look, here is my telephone number. Call me if you can visit Milan and come spend a couple of days with us.

Marco: With pleasure, and many thanks.

VOCABULARY

abbiamo parlato	we have spoken
avete	you have
casa (in)	home (at)
c'è	is
chi	that, what
chiamatemi	call me
città	city
coppie	couples
con	with
così bene	so well
da	of, from
dove	where
due	two
ecco	here is
è proprio così	that's right
figli	sons, children
forse	perhaps
francese	French
giorno, giorni	day, days
grazie	thanks
il fatto è	the fact is
in	in
inglese	English
io	I
Italiani	Italians
ma	but
mia, *f.*, -o, *m.*	my
medico	doctor
mi chiamo	my name is
Milano	Milan
mille	a thousand, many
moglie	wife

nati, *pl.*	born
noi	we, us
nostra, *f.*	our
numero	number
parenti	relatives
parlate	you speak
passare	to pass, spend
permettetemi	allow me
piacere	pleasure
piacere di conoscervi	pleased to meet you
presentarmi	to introduce myself
professore	professor, teacher
potete	you can
questa	he, this lady
se	if
sempre	always
siamo	we are
sì	yes
sentite	(you) listen, look
sposa	wife
stiamo ritornando	we are returning
sono	I am
telefono	telephone
tutti e due	the two of us
uno	one
venite	(you) come
visitare	to visit
visitato	visited
voi siete	you are
vuole dire	that means

LOCUZIONI — EXPRESSIONS

permettetemi di presentarmi	allow me to introduce myself
mi chiamo	my name is
piacere di conoscervi	glad to meet you
il fatto è	the fact is
vuole dire	that means
è proprio così	that's it, exactly
e voi che siete?	and what do you do?
ecco	here is
il mio numero di telefono	my telephone number
venite passare	come and spend
con piacere	with pleasure
mille grazie	many thanks

ESERCIZI — EXERCISES:

1. Copy the text, read it aloud and translate it.

2. Make up sentences with the following phrases and repeat them three times:
   Mi chiamo. Piacere di conoscervi. La nostra città.

3. Translate into Italian:
   Allow me to introduce myself.
   We were born in America.
   Many thanks.
   Are you Italians?

4. Translate into English:
   Ecco il mio numero di telefono.
   Abbiamo visitato parenti in America.
   Venite passare uno o due giorni con noi.
   Piacere di conoscervi.

5. Memorize these Italian names: Marco, Maria, Gianni, Anna.

GRAMMAR

II. Nouns

A. Gender

(a) **Masculine** — those ending in -o:
il ginocchio, *the knee*
il figlio, *the son*
(Exception: **la** mano, *the hand)*

(b) **Feminine** — those ending in -a: la figlia, *the daughter*
(Some exceptions: **il** telegramma, *the telegram*; **il** programma, *the program)*

— those ending in -**zione**, -**gione**, -**udine**:
l'azione, *the action*   la ragione, *the reason*
la prigione, *the prison*   la servit*u*dine, *service*

(c) **Masculine or Feminine** — a few ending in -e can be either:
il padre, *the father*   **il** fiume, *the river*
la madre, *the mother*   **la** pace, *the peace*

B. Number

Masculine nouns, whatever the ending, form their plural in -i.

il poeta, *the poet*   i poeti, *the poets*
il medico, *the doctor*   i medici, *the doctors*
il padre, *the father*   i padri, *the fathers*

(a) Masculine nouns ending in -ca and -ga form their plural in -chi (kee) and -ghi (ghee) respectively, in order to retain the original hard sound of the consonant.

il monarca, *the monarch*	i monarchi, *the monarchs*
il collega, *the colleague*	i colleghi, *the colleagues*
il lago, *the lake*	i laghi, *the lakes*

Some exceptions: -co > -ci

medico, *doctor*	medici, *doctors*
amico, *friend*	amici, *friends*
greco, *Greek*	greci, *Greeks*
nemico, *enemy*	nemici, *enemies*
porco, *pig*	porci, *pigs*

(b) The following masculine nouns, which end in -o, have an irregular plural in -a:

centinaio, *hundred*	centinaia, *hundreds*
miglio, *mile*	miglia, *miles*
migliaio, *thousand*	migliaia, *thousands*
paio, *pair*	paia, *pairs*
uovo, *egg*	uova, *eggs*

Feminine nouns form their plural in -e.

la strada, *the street*	le strade, *the streets*
la guancia, *the cheek*	le guance, *the cheeks*

Feminine nouns ending in -ca or -ga form their plural in -che and -ghe respectively, in order to retain the original hard sound of the consonant.

un' oca, *a goose*	tre oche, *three geese*
la fuga, *the flight*	le fughe, *the flights*

Nouns ending in -e, whether masculine or feminine, form their plural in -i.

la madre, *the mother*   le madri, *the mothers*
il padre, *the father*   i padri, *the fathers*
la lezione, *the lesson*   le lezioni, *the lessons*

Invariables - these are nouns that retain the same ending in the plural:

all monosyllables: — il re, *the king* — i re, *the kings*

all nouns ending in:

— i: il brindisi, *the toast* - i brindisi, *the toasts*
— an accented vowel: una città, *a city* - tre città, *three cities*
— a consonant: l'onnibus, *the bus* - gli onnibus, *the buses*

ESERCIZI — EXERCISES:

Translate the following into Italian:

1. A pair of eggs.

2. Mark and Gianni are friends.

3. Hundreds of miles.

4. The doctors are not Italians; they are Greek.

5. The brothers are colleagues.

LEZIONE TERZA

---·◆·---

LESSON THREE

L'ALBERGO

Marco: Questa prima colazione che l'albergo ci offre nella sala da pranzo è differente della nostra colazione in America.

Maria: È vero; qua ci danno pane e burro e conserva di frutta e caffè e latte.

Marco: Si, ma domane voglio provare il bar qua vicino, dove possiamo avere una spremuta di arancia, un cappuccino e un cornetto.

Maria: Una buona idea, Marco. Allora facciamo così.

Marco: Il nostro letto è comodo ma non ti pare strano avere la stanza da bagno con solo una doccia?

Maria: Strano davvero. Io preferisco lavarmi nella vasca da bagno, invece della doccia.

Marco: E io prefirisco la doccia.

Maria: Quanto ci fanno pagare per la stanza?

Marco: Sessanta mila lire. Non ti pare un prezzo discreto?

Maria: Davvero. Ma dimmi, quando ci ritorneranno i passaporti?

Marco: Oggi, disse l'albergatore.

Maria: Benissimo. Allora, continuamo il giro di Roma.

Marco: Sì, ma oggi il giro è a piedi.

THE HOTEL

Mark: This first breakfast the hotel is serving us in the dining room is quite different than ours in the States.

Mary: That's true. Here they give us bread and butter and fruit preserves and coffee and milk.

Mark: Yes, but tomorrow I want to try the nearby bar, where we can have freshly-squeezed orange juice, a cappuccino and a *cornetto*, that is a chocolate or custard-filled croissant.

Mary: A good idea, Mark. Let's do just that.

Mark: Our bed is comfortable, but don't you think our bathroom feels strange with only a shower?

Mary: Strange, indeed. I prefer to bathe in a bathtub instead of the shower.

Mark: I prefer the shower.

Mary: How much are we paying for our room?

Mark: Sixty thousand liras. Don't you think that's reasonable?

Mary: Yes, indeed. Tell me, when will they return our passports?

Mark: The hotelier said today.

Mary: Fine. Now let's continue our tour of Rome.

Mark: Yes, but today it will be on foot.

VOCABULARY

albergatore	hotelier
albergo	hotel
allora	then
arancia	oranges
avere	to have
bar	coffee shop
ben*i*ssimo	fine
buona, *f.*	good
burro	butter
caffè	coffee
cappuccino	cappuccino
ci	us
c*o*modo	comfortable
conserva di frutta	fruit preserves
continuamo	we continue
cornetto	filled croissant
così	just that
danno	they give
davvero	indeed, really
differente	different
dimmi	tell me
discreto	reasonable
disse	he, she said
doccia	shower
facciamo	we do, let's do
fanno	they make, do
idea	idea
invece di	instead of
io	I
latte	milk
lavarmi	to wash myself
letto	bed

ma	but
mila	thousand
nella	in the
offre	offers
oggi	today
per la	for the
pagare	to pay
pane	bread
pare	it seems
passaporti	passports
piedi, a	on foot
possiamo	we can
prefirisco	I prefer
prezzo	price
prima colazione	breakfast
provare	to try
qua	here
quando	when
quanto	how much
questa	this
ritorneranno	will return
sala da pranzo	dining room
sessanta	sixty
solo	only
spremuta	squeezed juice
stanza	room
stanza da bagno	bathroom
strano	strange
ti	to you
vasca da bagno	bathtub
vicino	near

LOCUZIONI — EXPRESSIONS

prima colazione	breakfast
sala da pranzo	dining room
conserva di frutta	fruit preserves
voglio provare	I want to try
qua vicino	nearby
spremuta di arancia	freshly-squeezed orange juice
una buona idea	a good idea
faciamo così	let's do just that
la stanza da bagno	the bathroom
strano davvero	strange, indeed
la vasca da bagno	the bathtub
quanto ci fanno pagare	how much do we have to pay
un prezzo discreto	a reasonable price
sì, davvero	yes, indeed
il giro è a piedi	the tour is on foot

ESERCIZI — EXERCISES:

1. Copy the text, read it aloud and translate it.

2. Make up sentences with the following phrases and repeat them
   three times:
   fare un giro a piedi; sì, davvero; prefirisco la doccia; un prezzo
   discreto

3. Translate into Italian:
   our bed is comfortable; I want to try the nearby bar; today the
   tour will be on foot; I prefer to bathe in a bathtub

4. Translate into English:
   non ti pare un prezzo discreto?; io prefirisco lavarmi nella vasca da
   bagno; io prefirisco la doccia; allora facciamo così

5. Memorize:
   continuamo il giro di Roma; il nostro letto è commodo; possiamo
   avere una spremuta di arancia; quanto ci fanno pagare per la
   stanza?

GRAMMAR

III. ADJECTIVES

Adjectives agree with their nouns in gender and number.

Il gatto è pulito	*The cat is neat*
Stanze pulite	*Clean rooms*
La ragazza è bella	*The little girl is pretty*

A. Gender and Number

Adjectives which end in -o are masculine and form their feminine in
-a. Singular adjectives which end in -e are invariable and have the same
ending in the masculine and feminine.

buono libro, *good book*	buona scarpa, *good shoe*
ragazzo felice, *happy boy*	ragazza felice, *happy girl*

Adjectives form their plural in the same way as nouns:
Masc.: -o to –i   Fem.: -a to –e   Masc. or Fem.: -e to -i

un bello zio, *a handsome uncle*	i begli zii, *the handsome uncles*
una buona ragazza, *a good girl*	le buone ragazze, *the good girls*
un cane grande, *a large dog*	i cani grandi, *the large dogs*

Adjectives of either gender or number may be used as a noun.

i buoni, *the good*	la bella, *the beautiful woman*

B. *Comparison*

(a) All adjectives form

— their comparative by prefixing **più**, *more*, to the adjective.

più bello, *more beautiful*
più grande, *bigger*

— their superlative, by prefixing the definite article (il, la) to the comparative.

il più bello, *the most beautiful*
il più grande, *the biggest*

(b) When the superlative immediately follows the noun, the definite article is omitted from **più**.

la vía **più** corta, *the shortest way*

(c) *Larger* and *smaller* (size) are **più** grande and **più** piccolo; *Older* and *younger* (age) are **maggiore** and **minore**.

La casa di Nino è la **più** grande. *Nino's house is the largest.*
Paolo è il fratello **più** piccolo.   *Paul is the smallest brother.*
Nino è il fratello **minore**.   *Nino is the youngest brother.*

(d) The adverb *less* is expressed by **meno**; *least* by **il (la) meno**.

Questa stanza è **la meno** bella. *This room is the least pretty.*

(e) The conjunction *than* is **che** when used to express comparison.

L'albergo è più grande **che** bello.
The hotel is larger than (it is) beautiful.

—But before a noun, a pronoun, or a numeral, *than* is rendered
by the preposition **di**.

Loro sono più ricchi **di** me.   *They are richer than I.*
Meno **di** cinque.   *Less than five.*

(f) *The more ... the more* is **più ... più**.
Più studio, **più** imparo.   *The more I study, the more I learn.*

(g) *The less ... the less* is **meno ... meno**.
Meno studio, **meno** imparo. *The less I study, the less I learn.*

ESERCIZI — EXERCISES:

Translate the following into Italian:

1. Paul is the oldest brother.

2. Nino is smaller than Paul.

3. This room is the largest.

4. Mary is more beautiful than Lola.

5. John is richer than I.

LEZIONE QUARTA

LESSON FOUR

DOMANDARE DIREZIONI

Marco:	Maria, questa spremuta d'arancia è molto saporita.
Maria:	D'accordo. E il cappuccino è delizioso. Adesso possiamo cominciare il giro a piedi, non è vero?
Marco:	Sì, ma prima bisogna domandare direzioni. *Al impiegato del bar.* Scusatemi, stiamo facendo un giro della città a piedi; mi saprà dire la direzione al Foro?
L'Impiegato:	È facile; quando uscite dall'albergo andate a sinistra a la Via Cavour che va direttamente al Foro Romano.
Marco:	Grazie. Andiamo, Maria. La carta stradale indica che possiamo anche vedere il Colosseo che è vicino al Foro.

Sono arrivati al Colosseo.

Maria:	Dicono che il Colosseo è il più gran monumento dei tempi romani dove c'erano spettacoli crudeli fra gladiatori e fra uomini e animali.

Dal Colosseo, vanno a piedi al Foro Romano.

Marco:	Queste statue fanno pensare che siamo stati trasportati ai tempi antichi.
Maria:	È vero, e se ti vesti in una toga, ti possiamo chiamare Senatore Marco.
Marco:	Sì, ma scherzi a parte, è tempo di trovare il piccolo ristorante qua vicino che l'albergatore ci ha raccomandato.

ASKING FOR DIRECTIONS

Mark:	Maria, this freshly squeezed orange juice is quite tasty.
Maria:	I agree, and the cappuccino is delicious. Now we can start our walking tour, can't we?
Mark:	Yes, but first we must ask for directions. *To the bar attendant.* Excuse me, we're touring the city on foot. Can you tell us how to get to the Forum?
The Attendant:	That's easy. When you leave the hotel, turn left into Via Cavour, which leads directly to the Forum.
Mark:	Thanks. Let's go, Maria. The street map shows that we can also see the Colosseum, which is near the Forum.

They have arrived at the Colosseum.

Maria:	They say that the Colosseum is the biggest monument of Roman times, where there were cruel spectacles between gladiators and between men and animals.

From the Colosseum, they go on foot to the Roman Forum.

Mark:	The statues make one think that we have been transported back to ancient times.
Maria:	That's true, and if you put on a toga, we can call you Senator Mark.
Mark:	Right, but joking aside, it's time to find the small restaurant nearby, which our hotelier recommended.

VOCABULARY

adesso	now
anche	also
andate	go
andiamo	we go, let us go
animali	animals
antico	old, ancient
bisogna	one must
cappuccino	cappuccino
carta stradale	street map
c'erano	there were
che	which, that
chiamare	to call
chiamata	called
ci	us, to us
cominciare	to begin
crudeli, *pl.*	cruel
d'accordo	agreed
delizioso	delicious
dicono	they say
direttamente	directly
direzioni	directions
domandare	to ask for
dove	where
facile	easy
fanno	they make
Foro	the Forum
fra	between
fresca, *f.*	fresh
gladiatori	gladiators
gran	great
ha	he, she has
impiegato	employee

*i*ndica	indicates
ma	but
mi saprà dire?	can you tell me?
monumento	monument
parte, a	apart, aside
pensare	to think
*pi*ccolo	small
più, il	the most
possiamo	we can
prima	first
qua	here
quando	when
queste, *f., pl.*	these
raccomandato	recommended
ristorante	restaurant
romano	Roman
saporita, *f.*	tasty
scherzi	jokes
scus*a*temi	excuse me
se	if
senatore	senator
siamo stati	we have been
sinistra, a	to the left
sono arrivati	they've arrived
spett*a*coli	spectacles
stiamo facendo	we are doing
statua	statue
tempo, -i	time, times
ti	you, yourself
toga	toga
trasportati	transported
trovare	find
*uo*mini	men
uscite	you leave
vanno	they go

vedere	see
vero	true
vesti	you dress
vicino	near, nearby

LOCUZIONI — EXPRESSIONS

d'accordo	agreed, I agree
non è vero?	isn't it so (true)?
bisogna domandare direzioni	we must ask for directions
mi saprà dire?	can you tell me?
è facile	that's easy
andate a sinistra	go to the left
la carta stradale	the street map
qua vicino	nearby here
scherzi a parte	joking aside
vanno a piedi	they go on foot

ESERCIZI — EXERCISES:

1. Copy the text, read it aloud and translate it.

2. Make up sentences with the following phrases and repeat them
   three times:
   andate a sinistra; mi saprà dire?; è facile; non è vero?; è vicino al
   Foro; un giro della città; scherzi a parte

3. Translate into Italian:
   of course, I agree; the cappuccino is delicious; cruel spectacles; if
   you dress up in a toga; nearby

4. Translate into English:
   una spremuta d'arancia; ma prima bisogna domandare direzioni;
   mi saprà dire?; fanno pensare di tempi antichi; scherzi a parte

5. Memorize:
   d'accordo; ai tempi antichi; è vero; il ristorante qua vicino;
   andate a sinistra; un giro della città a piedi; spettacoli crudeli
   fra gladiatori

GRAMMAR

IV. AUGMENTATIVES & DIMINUTIVES

Italian often uses a suffix to express size or quality. The suffix may be added to a noun, an adjective or an adverb.

Augmentatives

(a) The most common ending is *-issimo* (*f. -issima*), *very*, which is generally added only to adjectives and adverbs.

largo, (adj.) *wide*	largh*issimo, very wide*
grande, (adj.) *big*	grand*issimo, very big*
bene, (adv.) *well*	ben*issimo, very well*

(b) The principal suffix denoting largeness is -**one**; it is always masculine with only one rarely used exception.

bocca, *mouth*	un bocc**one**, *a mouthful*
casa, *house*	un cas**one**, *a large house*
boccia, *decanter*	una bocci**ona**, *a big decanter*

(c) The ending -*accio* denotes worthlessness.

roba, *stuff, goods*	rob**accia**, *trash*
tempo, *weather*	temp**accio**, *nasty weather*

Diminutives

(d) The most important suffixes denoting smallness are **-ino**, **-a**; **-etto**, **-a**; **-ello**, **-a**; and **-uccio**, **-a**.

sorella, *sister*	sorellina, *little sister*
bello, *beautiful*	bellino, *rather pretty*
piazza, *plaza*	piazzetta, *little plaza*
campana, *bell*	campanella, *little bell*
casa, *house*	casuccia, *a little house*
Gianni, *John*	Giannino, *Johnny*

ESERCIZI — EXERCISES:

Translate the following into Italian:

1. A mouthful of cappuccino.

2. The room is very wide.

3. Johnny is Mary's brother.

4. Johnny has a little sister.

5. The little house is Mary's.

6. It is a rather pretty little house.

LEZIONE QUINTA

---•---

LESSON FIVE

NEL RISTORANTE

Marco: Stamattina domandai all'albergatore il nome di un
            ristorante che specializza in pietanze romane, e mi dette
            il nome di una osteria qua vicino.

Maria: Come si chiama?

Marco: Osteria Romana. E disse che ci possiamo andare a piedi
            in un attimo.

Maria: Tutti e due abbiamo fame, dunque, avanti! Andiamo!

Dopo cinque minuti arrivano all'Osteria Romana.

Marco: Una tavola per due, per favore. *Quando sono seduti, il
            cameriere da loro la lista.* Cameriere, stasera vogliamo
            mangiare una pietanza romana. Che ci raccomanda?

Cameriere: Per cominciare, vi raccomando una pietanza speciale
            romana, Fettuccine Alfredo. Si prepara con fettuccine al
            dente, burro, formaggio parmigiano, e panna. Poi una
            insalata mista, e finalmente le pesche in vino.

Marco: Benissimo.

Cameriere: E per vino, forse un bicchiere di Frascati, il vino romano
            rinomato.

Marco: Ma certo.

*Quando hanno finito la cena, pagano il conto, pane e coperto, e una
mancia per il cameriere, e, contenti, tornano all'albergo.*

AT THE RESTAURANT

Mark: This morning I asked the hotelier for a restaurant that specializes in Roman foods and he gave me the name of a nearby restaurant.

Maria: What is it called?

Mark: Roman Tavern. He said that we can get there on foot in no time.

Maria: We're both hungry, so, forward march! Let's go!

They get to the Roman Tavern in five minutes.

Mark: A table for two, please. *When they are seated, the waiter gives them a menu.* Waiter, tonight we want to eat a Roman dish. What do you recommend?

Waiter: To begin with, I recommend a special Roman dish, Fettuccine Alfredo. It is prepared with *fettuccine al dente,* butter, parmigiano cheese, and cream. Then a mixed salad, and finally peaches in wine.

Mark: Fine.

Waiter: And as for wine, perhaps a glass of Frascati, the famous Roman wine.

Mark: Of course.

When they have finished, they pay the bill and cover and give the waiter a tip; then, quite content, they return to the hotel.

VOCABULARY

abbiamo	we have
andare	to go
andiamo	let's go
*a*ttimo	instant
avanti	forward (march)
ben*i*ssimo	fine, very good
bicchiere	glass
burro	butter
cameri*e*re	waiter
cena	dinner
certo (ma)	of course
chiama, si	it is called
ci	(to) us
ci	there
cinque	five
come	how, what, as to
cominciare	to begin
con	with
contenti	content, happy
conto	bill
da	he gives
dente (al)	firm to the bite
dette	he gave
disse	he said
domandai	I asked
due	two
dunque	(so) then
fame (abbiamo)	(we are) hungry
fettuccine	a wide pasta
finalmente	finally
finito	finished
formaggio	cheese

forse	perhaps
frascati	a Roman wine
insalata	salad
lista	menu
loro	to them
mancia	tip
mangiare	to eat
minuti	minutes
mista	mixed
nome	name
osteria	tavern
pagano	they pay
pane e coperto	cover
panna	cream
parmigiano	parmesan
perciò	therefore
per favore	please
pietanza	dish
poi	then
per	to, for
pesche	peaches
possiamo	we can
prepara (si)	it is prepared
qua	here
quando	when
raccomanda	recommend(s)
rinomato	renowned
ristorante	restaurant
romano (a)	Roman
seduti (sono)	seated (they are)
speciale	special
specializza	specializes
stamattina	this morning
stasera	tonight
tavola	table

tornano	they return
tutti e due	both of us
vi	(to) you
vino	wine
vicino	near
vogliamo	we want (to)

LOCUZIONI — EXPRESSIONS

pietanze romane	Roman dishes
qua vicino	nearby
in un attimo	in an instant
avanti	forward (march)
andiamo	let us go
Osteria Romana	Roman Tavern
una tavola per due	a table for two
per favore	please
che ci raccomanda?	what do you recommend?
per cominciare	to begin with
una insalata mista	a mixed salad
pagano il conto	they pay the bill
pane e coperto	cover (bread and tableware)
una mancia per il cameriere	a tip for the waiter
pesche in vino	peaches in wine
un bicchiere di frascati	a glass of Frascati wine

Esercizi — Exercises:

1. Copy the text, read it aloud and translate it.

2. Make up sentences with the following phrases and repeat them three times:
   pagano il conto; pietanze romane; qua vicino; in un *a*ttimo

3. Translate into Italian:
   Let's go!; we want to eat some Roman food; I recommend a special Roman dish; the waiter gives them a menu

4. Translate into English:
   tutti e due abbiamo fame; una mancia per il cameriere; che ci raccomanda?; una *t*avola per due

5. Memorize:
   pane e coperto; in un *a*ttimo; una mancia per il cameriere; andiamo; una insalata mista

GRAMMAR

V. NUMERALS

The Cardinals

1 uno	11 *u*ndici	30 trenta
2 due	12 d*o*dici	40 quaranta
3 tre	13 tr*e*dici	50 cinquanta
4 quattro	14 quattordici	60 sessanta
5 cinque	15 qu*i*ndici	70 settanta
6 sei	16 s*e*dici	80 ottanta
7 sette	17 diciasette	90 novanta
8 otto	18 diciotto	100 cento
9 nove	19 diciannove	200 duecento
10 dieci	20 venti	300 trecento

1,000 mille — 2,000 due mila — 1,000,000 un milione

Uno has a feminine, una; when used as an adjective, it has the same forms as the indefinite article.

una cosa, *one thing*

The plural of **mille** is **mila** as in **due mila.**

due mila case, *two thousand houses*

1. Unlike English, no conjunction is used between the different parts of a number — **duecento quaranta,** *two hundred and forty*

   Nor is an indefinite article used before **cento** and **mille.**
   — **cento libri,** *a hundred books,* **mille dollari,** *a thousand dollars*

2. *Both, all three,* etc. are **tutti e** due, **tutti e** tre, etc.

3. *What time is it?* is **che ora è?** or **che ore sono?** *It is six,* etc., is **sono le sei,** etc. (**ore,** *hour,* being understood.)

Sono le due e mezzo.	*It is half past two.*
Sono le tre e dieci.	*It is ten minutes past three.*
Ci mancano venti minuti alle quattro.	*It is twenty minutes to four.*
Sono le cinque meno un quarto.	*It is a quarter to five.*

The Ordinals

1st	**primo**	8th	**ottavo**
2nd	**secondo**	9th	**nono**
3rd	**terzo**	10th	**decimo**
4th	**quarto**	20th	**ventesimo**
5th	**quinto**	30th	**trentesimo**
6th	**sesto**	100th	**centesimo**
7th	**settimo**	1,000th	**millesimo**

All ordinals form their feminine and plural like other adjectives which end in **-o.**

La terza figlia si chiama Carla.	*The third daughter is called Carla.*
Questa è la quinta lezione.	*This is the fifth lesson.*

(a) Ordinal numerals are used after the names of rulers, without the article.

Carlo **Secondo**	*Charles the Second*
Piu **Nono**	*Pius IX*

(b) For the day of the month, except the first, a cardinal number is used.

cinque d'aprile	*the fifth of April*
il primo di maggio	*the first of May*

(c) *A couple* or *a pair* is **un paio**; *the plural is* **paia**.

un paio di scarpe	*a pair of shoes*
due paia di scarpe	*two pairs of shoes*

(d) The **-ina** suffix indicates *about, some,* as in **una diecina, una ventina, una trentina,** etc., but **una dozzina** is *a dozen*.

una cinquantina di libbri	*some fifty books*
una dozzina di libbri	*a dozen books*

(e) *Once, twice,* etc. are **una volta, due volte,** etc.

Venne alla casa **tre volte**.　　*He came to the house three times.*

(f) *Several times* is **parecchie volte.**

L'ho visto **parecchie volte**.　　*I have seen it several times.*

Esercizi — Exercises:

Translate the following into Italian:

1. Some thirty houses.

2. Two pairs of shoes.

3. Maria has two dozen books.

4. It is 4:30.

5. The sixth of May.

6. Two thousand one hundred.

LEZIONE SESTA

LESSON SIX

GIRAR LE BOTTEGHE

Maria: Marco, che ti pare - oggi possiamo girar le botteghe?

Marco: Perchè no? Dove vuoi andare prima?

Maria: A un negozio di vestiario.

Marco: Allora, andiamo.

Nel negozio.

Maria: *All'impiegata.* Vorrei vedere una veste elegante in blu.

L'Impiegata: Ecco, una bellissima.

Maria: La posso provare?

L'Impiegata: Ma certo.

Maria: *Dopo averla provato.* Mi sta bene. Marco, ti piace?

Marco: Sì, mi piace assai.

Maria: Quanto costa?

L'Impiegata: Ottantacincque mila lire.

Maria: È troppo cara... Non ti pare, Marco?

Marco: Sì, ma è una bella veste e pagheremo il prezzo. *Pagano il cassiere ed escono dal negozio.* E adesso dove vuoi andare, Maria?

Maria:	Vorrei andare alla farmac*i*a che è qua vicino. *Nella farmacia, al farmacista.* Ho bisogno di aspirina, di una bottiglia di acqua dentifr*i*cia per sciacquare la bocca, e di un tubetto di pasta dentifr*i*cia.
Farmacista:	Niente di più?
Marco:	Io ho bisogno di un tubetto di crema per la barba.
Farmacista:	*Dopo cinque minuti.* Ecco.

Marco paga ed escono dalla farmacia.

Marco:	E adesso dove vuoi andare, Maria?
Maria:	Vorrei andare a una sala di bellezza.
Marco:	Ma tu sei così bella che non hai bisogno di sala di bellezza.
Maria:	E tu, Marco, sempre che scherzi.
Marco:	Ecco la sala di bellezza, bella.

Entrano e Maria parla con il gerente.

Maria:	Quando posso venire per un' ondulazione permanente?
Il Gerente:	Può venire domane alle nove?
Maria:	Sì, mille grazie.

SHOPPING AROUND

Maria:	Mark, what do you think? Can we go shopping today?
Mark:	Why not? Where do you want to go first?
Maria:	To a dress shop.
Mark:	Well, then, let's go.

At the shop.

Maria:	*To the saleslady.* I'd like to see a stylish blue dress.
The Saleslady:	Here you are. A beauty.
Maria:	May I try it on?
The Saleslady:	Of course.
Maria:	*After having tried it on.* It looks good on me. Do you like it, Mark?
Mark:	Yes, I like it very much.
Maria:	How much does it cost?
The Saleslady:	85,000 liras.
Maria:	That's too expensive... Don't you think so, Mark?
Mark:	Yes, but it's a beautiful dress and we'll pay the price. *They pay the cashier and leave the store.* Where do we go now, Maria?

Maria:	I'd like to go to the drugstore which is nearby. *At the drugstore, to the pharmacist.* I need aspirins, a bottle of mouthwash to rinse my mouth, and a tube of toothpaste.
Pharmacist:	Nothing else?
Mark:	I need a tube of shaving cream.
Pharmacist:	*After five minutes.* There you are.

Mark pays and they leave the pharmacy.

Mark:	Where do you want to go now, Maria?
Maria:	I must find a beauty parlor.
Mark:	But you're so beautiful that you don't need a beauty parlor.
Maria:	Mark, you're always joking.
Mark:	Here's the beauty parlor, beautiful.

They enter and Maria speaks with the manager.

Maria:	When can I come for a permanent?
The Manager:	Can you come tomorrow at nine?
Maria:	Yes, many thanks.

VOCABULARY

acqua dentifricia	mouthwash
allora	well, then
andare	to go
andiamo	we (let us) go
aspirina	aspirin
assai	a lot
bella	beautiful
bellissima	very beautiful
bene	well
bisogno, ho (hai)	I (you) need
blu	blue
bocca	mouth
botteghe	shops
bottiglia	bottle
cara	dear, expensive
cassiere	cashier
certo (ma)	of course
cinque	five
crema per la barba	shaving cream
con	with
così	so (very)
costa	it costs
e, ed	and
dalla	from the
di	of
domane	tomorrow
dopo	after
dove	where
ecco	here you are
elegante	stylish
entrano	they enter
escono	they leave

farmac*i*a	drugstore
farmacista	pharmacist
gerente	manager
girar(e)	tour
hai	you have
impiegata, *f.*	employee
ma	but
mila	thousand
mille grazie	many thanks
minuti	minutes
negozio	shop
niente di più	nothing else
nove (alle)	at nine o'clock
ondulazione permanente	a permanent
ottantacinque	eighty-five
paga	(he) pays
pagano	they pay
pagheremo	we'll pay
pare (ti)	seems to you
parla	he, she speaks
pasta dentifr*i*cia	toothpaste
per	for, to
piace	you like
piace (mi)	I like it
perchè	why
possiamo	we can
posso	I can
prezzo	price
prima	first
provare	to try
provato	tried
quando	when
quanto	how much
sala di bellezza	beauty parlor
scherzi	you joke

sciacquare	to rinse
sei (tu)	you are
sempre	always
sta	is, fits, looks
troppo	too much
tubetto	tube
vedere	to see
venire	to come
veste	dress
vestiario	clothing
vorrei	I would want
vuoi	you want

LOCUZIONI — EXPRESSIONS

che ti pare?	what do you think?
girar le botteghe	to go shopping
un negozio di vestiario	a dress shop
una veste elegante	a stylish dress
la posso provare?	may I try it on?
mi sta bene	it looks good on me
ti piace?	do you like it?
mi piace assai	I like it very much
quanto costa?	how much does it cost?
è troppo cara	it's too expensive
non ti pare?	don't you think so?
pagheremo il prezzo	we'll pay the price
escono dal negozio	they leave the shop
è qua vicino	it's nearby
una bottiglia di acqua dentifricia	a bottle of mouthwash
per sciacquare la bocca	to rinse the mouth
un tubetto di pasta dentifricia	a tube of toothpaste
niente di più?	nothing else?
crema di barba	shaving cream
una sala di bellezza	a beauty parlor
sempre che scherzi	you're always joking
parla col gerente	she speaks with the manager
una ondulazione permanente	a permanent

ESERCIZI — EXERCISES:

1. Copy the text, read it aloud and translate it.

2. Make up sentences with the following phrases and repeat them three times:
   niente di più?; un tubetto di pasta dentifricia; quanto costa?; girar le botteghe

3. Translate into Italian:
   Mark, you're always joking; when can I come for a permanent?; it looks good on me; they leave the shop

4. Translate into English:
   una veste elegante; la posso provare?; una sala di bellezza; una bottiglia di acqua dentifricia

5. Memorize:
   che ti pare?; girar le botteghe; sempre che scherzi; una sala di bellezza; quanto costa?

GRAMMAR

VI. PRONOUNS

Personal Pronouns

There are two types of personal pronouns:
disjunctive and **conjunctive**.

A. Disjunctive Pronouns

These pronouns do not receive the action of the verb:
as it were, they are <u>dis</u>-joined from it.

There are two types of disjunctives:

1. *Subject Pronouns*, used as the subject of a verb
2. *Object Pronouns*, used only after prepositions

1. Subject Pronouns

These are used as the subject of a verb.

Singular	Plural
<u>io</u> **parlo**, *I speak*	<u>noi</u> **parliamo**, *we speak*
<u>tu</u> **parli**, *you speak*	<u>voi</u> **parlate**, *you speak*
<u>egli</u> **parla**, *he (it) speaks*	<u>loro</u> *m.*, **parlano**, *they speak*
<u>lei</u> **parla**, *she (it) speaks*	<u>loro</u> *f.*, **parlano**, *they speak*

The familiar **tu** form is used in addressing children, relatives, close
friends, servants, and persons of a lower social rank.

The subject pronouns are generally omitted, but are always used for clarity and emphasis.

Parliamo chiaramente.   *We speak clearly.*
Lo faccio **io**, non lui.   *I do it, not he.*

2. Object Pronouns

These are used as the *object of a preposition*: **per lui**, *for him,* **a lei**, *to her.*

me, me   noi, us
te, you   voi, you
lui, him, it   loro, them, *m.*
lei, her, it   loro, them, *f.*

Filippo viene con **me**.   *Philip comes with me.*
Lo fa per **noi**.   *He does it for us.*
Te lo do.   *I give it to you.*

B. Conjunctive Pronouns

Conjunctive pronouns serve as the *direct object of a verb* (d.o.) and as the *indirect object without a preposition* (i.o.). These forms are so-called because they precede, join with, or follow the verb (**con-**, with: **junct-**, join).

Singular		Plural	
(d.o.)	(i.o.)	(d.o.)	(i.o.)
mi, *me*	me, *to me*	ci, *us*	ce, *to us*
ti, *you*	te, *to you*	vi, *you*	ve, *to you*
lo, *him*	gli, *to him*	li, *them*	loro, *to them* (m.)
la, *her*	gli, *to her*	le, *them*	loro, *to them* (f.)

Singular

(d.o.) **Mi** guarda.	*He looks at me.*
(i.o.) Maria **mi** da il libro.	*Mary gives me the book.*
Maria **melo** da.	*Mary gives it to me.*
(d.o.) **Ti** conosce.	*He knows you.*
(i.o.) Filippo **ti** da il libro.	*Philip gives you the book.*
Filippo **telo** da.	*Philip gives it to you.*
(d.o.) **Lo** (**la**) vedo qua.	*I see him (her) here.*
(i.o.) **Gli** parlo chiaramente.	*I speak to him (her) clearly.*

Plural

(d.o.) Mamma **ci** vuole bene.	*Mama loves us.*
(i.o.) Egli **ci** parla con sincerità.	*He speaks to us sincerely.*
(d.o.) Carlo **vi** guarda.	*Charles looks at you.*
(i.o.) Anna **velo** da.	*Anna gives it to you.*
(d.o.) **Li** amo.	*I love them.*
(i.o.) Date **loro** le mele.	*Give them the apples.*

1. Reflexive pronouns are conjunctive:

mi, *myself*	**ci**, *ourselves*
ti, *yourself*	**vi**, *yourselves*
si, *himself, herself*	**si**, *themselves* (m., f.)

Mi vesto. *I dress myself.*	**Ci** vestiamo. *We dress ourselves.*
Ti vesti. *You dress yourself.*	**Vi** vestite. *You dress yourselves.*
Si veste. *He, she dresses himself, herself.*	**Si** vestono. *They dress themselves.*

2. Another conjunctive pronoun is **ne**: *of it, of them, any, some, some of them.*

Non **ne** abbiamo.	*We don't have any.*
Ne volete?	*Do you want any?*

3. Conjunctive pronouns immediately precede the verb:

Mi vedete.	*You see me.*
Non **lo** capisco.	*I don't understand him.*

But when the verb is (a) *an infinitive* (inf.), (b) *a positive imperative* (pos. imp.), or (c) *a present participle* (pres. part.), *the pronoun follows the verb and is written with it as one word.*

(inf.)   (a) per veder**lo**, *to see him*
                      aver**lo** visto, *to have seen him*
(pos. imp.) (b) ved**eteli**, *see them*
                      dam**melo**, *give it to me*
(pres. part.) (c) avend**oci** visto, *having seen us*
                      vend**endoci**, *seeing us*

4. The conjunctive pronouns **me, te, gli, ce** and **ve** precede **lo, la** and **li** and unite with them.

Melo dice.	*He tells it to me.*
Tela conta (questa storia).	*He tells it to you (this tale).*
Glieli da.	*He gives them to them.*
Celi vende.	*He sells them to us.*
Veli mando.	*I send them to you.*

ESERCIZI — EXERCISES:

Translate the following into Italian:

1. We dress ourselves.

2. He does it for me.

3. Give it to me.

4. I don't want it.

5. He gives them to you.

6. Do you want any?

7. Carl gives me the book.

8. She dresses herself.

9. They speak.

LEZIONE SETTIMA

LESSON SEVEN

IN CAMINO

Marco: Questa è una bella macchina che Hertz ci ha fatto prenotare negli Stati Uniti. Ho la patente di guida internazionale e adesso possiamo cominciare il nostro viaggio a Milano, dove fummo invitati a passare due giorni con Gianni e Anna Orlando. Ma prima, in camino, visiteremo Firenze.

Maria: Quanto costa il noleggio della macchina?

Marco: È caro; tre cento cinquanta dollari alla settimana. Anche la benzina è cara — un dollaro e venti cinque al litro. E poi dobbiamo pagare una tassa di quasi cinque dollari per viaggiare nelle autostrade da una città principale all' altra. Insomma, è un poco caro, ma vale la pena, non ti pare?

Maria: Ma certo. Dunque, avanti... in camino.

Dopo tre ore di viaggio, arrivano a Firenze.

Marco: Ecco Firenze, Maria, la capitale culturale dell'Italia, la città di Dante, Petrarca e dei più famosi artisti del mondo, come Michelangelo e Leonardo da Vinci.

All'albergo si sono riposati in una bella camera a due letti e con bagno. Siccome è già mezzogiorno, vanno a un ristorante là vicino, dove domandano al cameriere quale è il piatto del giorno.

Il Cameriere: Oggi il piatto del giorno è trippa fiorentina.

Marco: Benissimo. Allora, trippa fiorentina per due.

ON THE ROAD

Mark: This is a nice car that Hertz had us reserve back in the
                States. I have an international driver's license and so
                now we can begin our trip to Milano, where we were
                invited to spend a couple of days with Gianni and
                Anna Orlando. But first we shall visit Florence on
                the way.

Maria: How much does the car rental cost?

Mark: It's expensive: three hundred and fifty dollars a week.
                Gas is expensive, too — a dollar and a quarter a liter.
                Then we have to pay a toll of almost five dollars on the
                highways between principal cities. In short, it's a bit
                expensive, but it's worthwhile, don't you think?

Maria: I certainly do... Well, then, we're on our way... Let's hit
                the road.

After a three-hour trip, they arrive in Florence.

Mark: We're in Florence, Maria, Italy's cultural capital, the
                city of Dante, Petrarch and of the world's most famous
                artists, like Michelangelo and Leonardo da Vinci.

*At the hotel they rest in a lovely room with twin beds and bath. Since it
is already noon, they go to a nearby restaurant, where they ask the waiter
what today's special dish is.*

The Waiter: Today we're featuring Tripe à la Florentine.

Mark: Fine. Florentine tripe for two, then.

VOCABULARY

a	to, at
alla settimana	a week
allora	then
altra, *f.*	another
anche	also
arrívano	they arrive
artisti	artists
autostrade	roads, highways
avanti	forward
bagno	bath
bella	beautiful
benzina	gasoline
*c*amera	room
camino (in)	on the road
capitale	capital
caro	expensive
certo (ma)	of course
città	city
cominciare	to begin
con	with
costa	costs
culturale	cultural
da	from
di	of
dobbiamo	we must
d*o*llari	dollars
dom*a*ndano	they ask
dopo	after
dove	where
due	two
dunque	well then
ecco	here is

famosi	famous
fiorentina, f.	Florentine
Firenze	Florence
fummo	we were
già	already
giorno	day
guida	driver's
insomma	in short, then
internazionale	international
invitati	invited
là vicino	nearby
letti	beds
litro	liter
ma	but
macchina	auto, car
mezzogiorno	noon
mondo	world
negli	in the
noleggio	rent
nostro, m.	our
oggi	today
ora, -e	hour, -s
pagare	to pay
pare (ti)	think so (you)
passare	to spend
patente	license
per	for, to
Petrarca	Petrarch
piatto	dish
più	more, most
poco	a bit, somewhat
poi	then
possiamo	we can
prenotare	to reserve
prima	before, first

principale	principal
quale è	what is
quanto	how much
quasi	almost
siccome	since
si sono riposati	they rested
Stati Uniti	United States
tassa	tax, toll
tre	three
tre cento cinquanta	350
trippa	tripe
un dollaro e venti cinque	$1.25
vale	is worth
vanno	they go
viaggio	trip
visiteremo	we shall visit

LOCUZIONI — EXPRESSIONS

la patente di guida internazionale	international driver's license
fummu invitati	we were invited
quanto costa?	how much does it cost?
il noleggio della machina	the car rental
è un poco caro	it's somewhat expensive
vale la pena	it's worthwhile
non ti pare?	don't you think so?
dunque	well, then
dopo tre ore di viaggio	after traveling three hours
si sono riposati	they rested
là vicino	nearby

Esercizi — Exercises:

1. Copy the text, read it aloud and translate it.

2. Make up sentences with the following phrases and repeat them
three times:
il noleggio della machina; non ti pare?; il piatto del giorno; la
patente di guida internazionale; vale la pena.

3. Translate into Italian:
it's a bit expensive; Florentine tripe for two; today's special dish;
after traveling three hours; don't you think so?

4. Translate into English:
è una bella machina; vale la pena; il piatto del giorno; una bella
camera a due letti; è già mezzogiorno.

5. Memorize:
non ti pare?; quanto costa?; il noleggio della machina; il piatto del
giorno; la patente di guida internazionale.

GRAMMAR

VII. ADJECTIVES AND PRONOUNS

A. Demonstrative Adjectives and Pronouns
agree in number and gender with the noun they modify or represent.

Adjectives   Pronouns

(a) *Near the speaker:* <u>this</u>; <u>this one</u>

questo (m.), questi (m., pl.), questa (f.), queste (f., pl.)

questo libro, *this book*	questo, *this one*
questa donna, *this woman*	questa, *this one*
questi ragazzi, *these boys*	questi, *these*
queste mele, *these apples*	queste, *these*

(b) *Near the person addressed:* <u>that</u>; <u>that one</u>

codesto (m.), codesti (m., pl.), codesta (f.), codeste (f., pl.)

codesto libro, *that book*   codesto, *that one*
                           etc.

(c) *Away from the speaker or the person addressed:* <u>that</u>; <u>that one</u>

<u>quello</u>, quel (m.), <u>quelli</u>, quegli (pl.), quella (f.), quelle (pl.)
<u>quello</u> (s.), <u>quegli</u> (pl.) before s+consonant or z

quel libro, *that book* (*over there*) quello, *that one*
                           etc.

B. Interrogatives

1. The interrogative *who, whom* is **chi**, and *what* is **che**; both are invariable.

Chi verrà stasera?	*Who is coming tonight?*
A chi vedo?	*Whom do I see?*
Che fai?	*What are you doing?*

2. *Which?* is **quale, -li**; *how much?*, *how many?* is **quanto.**

Quale libro comprasti?	*Which book did you buy?*
Quali libri comprasti?	*Which books did you buy?*
Quanti soldi guadagnasti?	<u>*How much*</u> *money did you earn?*
Quante donne ci sono?	<u>*How many*</u> *women are there?*

C. Relative Pronouns

The principal relative pronouns are **che, cui, il quale, la quale, quale, i quali, le quali**: they apply to both persons and things, and mean *who, whom, which,* or *that.* **Che** and **cui** are invariable: in general **che** is used only as subject and direct object, **cui** only after prepositions or as an indirect object.

La lingua **che** parliamo.	*The language we speak.*
L'uomo **del quale** parlo.	*The man of whom I speak.*
Le persone **a cui** parlo.	*The persons to whom I speak.*

D. *Possessive Adjectives and Pronouns*

	Singular		Plural	
	MASC.	FEM.	MASC.	FEM.
my, mine:	il m*i*o	la m*i*a	i mi*e*i	le m*i*e
your, yours:	il t*u*o	la t*u*a	i tu*o*i	le t*u*e
his, her(s):	il s*u*o	la s*u*a	i su*o*i	le s*u*e
our, ours:	il nostro	la nostra	i nostri	le nostre
your, yours:	il vostro	la vostra	i vostri	le vostre
their, theirs:	il loro	la loro	i loro	le loro

Loro (their, theirs) is invariable (i.e. it does not agree with the noun in number and gender). The others <u>do</u> agree with the noun in number and gender.

> **il mio** libro, *my book.*
> **la sua** figlia, *his daughter*
> **le loro** figlie, *their daughters*
> **la nostra** madre, *our mother*
> è **la loro**, *she is theirs*

Esercizi — Exercises:

Translate the following into Italian:

1. Our daughter is beautiful.

2. This book is his.

3. The man to whom I speak.

4. Who is speaking?

5. That woman (over there) is beautiful.

6. Our mother and theirs.

7. How much money does it cost?

8. Whom do you see?

9. This one is good.

LEZIONE OTTAVA

LESSON EIGHT

FIRENZE

Marco: Maria, *eccoci* nella Piazza della Signoria, il centro più famoso di Firenze, la capitale del Rinascimento.

Maria: Sì, adesso che vedo queste belle *statue* e pitture, capisco perchè Firenze è così rinomata.

Marco: Senti, io direi che Firenze è la capitale culturale del mondo.

Maria: D'accordo. Guarda *Il Davide*, questa statua magnifica di Michelangelo, e *Il Marzocco* di Donatello. E la statua imponente di Cosimo I, il primo Medici.

Marco: E guarda qua nella Loggia della Signoria, *Il Perseo* di Benvenuto Cellini. Quando torniamo in casa, voglio rileggere la sua autobiografia.

Sono entrati nella Galleria degli Uffizi.

Maria: Dio! Che tesori! *La Primavera* di Botticelli, le pitture di Cimabue e di Giotto gli araldi del Rinascimento!

Marco: *La Madonna* di Raffaello, *Il Doni Tondo* di Michelangelo.

Maria: E *La Flora* di Tiziano! Tutti i giganti del Rinascimento.

Marco: Troppo, è davvero troppo. Non ne posso più. Basta per oggi. Non ti pare?

Maria: D'accordo, Marco. È tempo già di andar mangiar una delle famose bistecche fiorentine.

Marco: Una bella idea. Avanti.

FLORENCE

Mark: Maria, here we are in the Piazza della Signoria, the most famous center of Florence, the capital of the Renaissance.

Maria: Yes, now that I see these beautiful statues and paintings, I can understand why Florence is so famous.

Mark: Listen, I think Florence is the cultural capital of the world.

Maria: I agree. Look at the *David,* this magnificent Michelangelo statue, and Donatello's *Marzocco.* And the imposing statue of Cosimo I, the first Medici.

Mark: And look here in the Loggia della Signoria, Benvenuto Cellini's *Perseus.* When we get back home, I want to reread his autobiography.

They have entered the Galleria degli Uffizi.

Maria: Good Lord! What treasures! Botticelli's *Spring,* the paintings of Cimabue and Giotto, the heralds of the Renaissance!

Mark: Raphael's *Madonna*, Michelangelo's *Doni Tondo.*

Maria: And Titian's *Flora!* All the giants of the Renaissance.

Mark: Too much, really too much. I can't take anymore. Enough for today. Don't you agree?

Maria: I do, Mark. It's time to have one of those famous Florentine steaks.

Mark: A good idea. We're on our way.

VOCABULARY

araldi	heralds
autobiografia	autobiography
basta	enough
belle, *f., pl.*	beautiful
bistecca, -cche	beefsteak, -s
capisco	I understand
capitale	capital
casa	home
centro	center
così	so very
davvero	really
Dio	Good Lord
direi, io	I would say
eccoci	here we are
fiorentini, *m., pl.*	Florentine
giganti	giants
guarda	look
imponente	imposing
magnifica, *f.*	magnificent
mangiar (e)	to eat
mondo	world
oggi	today
perchè	why
pitture	paintings
posso	I can
primo	first
queste, *f., pl.*	these
rileggere	reread
Rinascimento	Renaissance
rinomata, *f.*	renowned
senti	listen
statua, -e	statue, -s

tesoro, -i	treasure, -s
torniamo	we return
troppo	too much
tutti	all
vedo	I see
voglio	I want

LOCUZIONI — EXPRESSIONS

eccoci	here we are
è così rinomata	it is so well-known
senti	listen
la capitale culturale	the cultural capital
d'accordo	agreed, I agree
guarda	look
questa statua magnifica	this magnificent statue
quando torniamo in casa	when we return home
Dio	Good Lord
che tesori!	what treasures!
davvero troppo	too much, really
non ne posso più	I can't take anymore
basta per oggi	enough for today
non ti pare?	don't you think so?
una bella idea	a good idea

ESERCIZI — EXERCISES:

1. Copy the text, read it aloud and translate it.

2. Make up sentences with the following phrases and repeat them three times:
   è davvero troppo; non ti pare?; basta per oggi; una bella idea; è così rinomata.

3. Translate into Italian:
   giants of the Renaissance; really too much; I can't take anymore; a good idea; don't you think so?

4. Translate into English:
   che tesori!; non ne posso più; davvero troppo; guarda; le famose bistecche fiorentini.

5. Memorize:
   non ti pare?; senti; guarda; basta per oggi; una bella idea.

GRAMMAR

VIII. Indefinite Adjectives, Pronouns, Conjunctions and Prepositions

A. Indefinite Adjectives & Pronouns

(a) _Si_, as an indefinite pronoun, used as the subject of a verb, is translated as *one, people, we, you,* or *they.*

Si mangia bene in Italia.	*One eats well in Italy.*
Si fa così.	*You do it this way.*

(b) _Ne,_ meaning *any of it, any of them.*

Non **ne** ho.	*I haven't any.*
Non **ne** ha più.	*He doesn't have any anymore.*
Ne avete?	*Do you have any?*

— When it really adds nothing to the meaning, it is omitted:

Non ha libri.	*He doesn't have (any) books.*
Volete vino?	*Do you want any wine?*

(c) *l'uno e l'altro* is translated as *both.*

Vuoi salsiccia o due uova?	*Do you want sausages or two eggs?*
L'uno e l'altro.	*Both (one and the other).*

(d) The following are some common indefinite pronouns (pron.) and
adjectives (adj.) or both (a reference list):

anybody, **qualcuno,** pron.

anything, **qualchecosa,** pron.

both, **tutti e due,** pron.

each, every, **ogni, ognuno,** both

either, **l'uno o l'altro,** both

everybody, **ognuno,** pron.

everything, **tutto,** pron.

few, a few, **pochi,** both

little, **poco,** both

less, **meno,** both

many, several, **parecchi, -e,** both

more, **più,** both

neither, **nè l'uno nè
l'altro,** pron.

nobody, **nessuno,** both

nothing, **niente,** adj., adv.

somebody, **qualcuno,** pron.

something, **qualchecosa,** pron.

B. Conjunctions and Prepositions (a reference list)

Conjunctions

Some common conjunctions are:

after, **dopo che**

although, **benchè**

and, **e**

as, **come**

as (since), **siccome, poichè**

because, **perchè**

before, **prima che**

but, **ma**

if, **se**

neither...nor, **nè...nè**

nor, **nè**

or, **o**

rather, **anzi**

since (causal), **siccome, giacchè**

so, **dunque**

so that, **di modo che**

than, that, **che**

that (in order that), **perchè**

then, **dunque**

therefore, **dunque, però, perciò**

unless, **a meno che non**

when, **quando**

whence, from where, **donde**

where, **dove**

whether, **se**

while, **mentre, mentre che**

Prepositions

Some common prepositions are:

about (approximately), **circa**	*in*, **in**
about (around), **intorno a**	*in front of*, **davanti a**
above, **sopra**	*inside of*, **dentro di**
according to, **secondo**	*instead of*, **invece di**
after, **dopo**	*in the midst of*, **in mezzo a**
against, **contra, contro**	*into*, **in, dentro di**
along, **lungo**	*near*, **vicino a**
among, **fra, tra**	*of*, **di**
as far as, **sino a, fino a**	*on, over*, **su, sopra**
as to, **quanto a**	*opposite*, **dirimpetto**
before (time), **prima di**	*out of, outside of*, **fuori di**
behind, **dietro**	*all round*, **intorno intorno**
below, under, **sotto**	*toward*, **verso**
between, within, **fra**	*through*, **per**
by means of, **per mezzo di**	*up to*, **sino a, fino a**
during, **durante**	*with*, **con**
except, **eccetto, tranne**	*without*, **senza**
from, **da, fin da**	*without (outside of)*, **fuori di**

Note the following uses:

1. *To* is omitted before an infinitive following an auxiliary verb:

Dovrebbe capire.	*He ought <u>to</u> understand.*
Possiamo venire.	*We'll be able <u>to</u> come.*
Non sa che fare.	*He doesn't know what <u>to</u> do.*

2. Only an infinitive may be used as the object of a preposition and not the present participle as in English.

Si fece capire senza <u>parlare</u>.   *He made himself understood without <u>speaking</u>.*

3. The preposition **da** has varied meanings:

(a) <u>Characteristic of</u>:
La sala **da** pranzo.   *The dining room.*

(b) <u>from</u>:
Arrivò oggi **da** Parigi.   *He arrived from Paris today.*

(c) <u>by</u>:
Fu fatto **da** Nino.   *It was done by Nino.*

(d) **Da** corresponds to English *on, at,* or *to* before the word *side,* and *as far as one is concerned:*
Da questa parte,   *On this side,*
Da sua parte, Gianni...   *As far as he's concerned, John...*

(e) <u>as a</u>:
Prometto **da** uomo d'onore.   *I promise as a man of honor.*

(f) <u>to</u>, indicating duty or necessity:
Ha qualchecosa **da** fare.   *He has something to do.*

Esercizi — Exercises:

Translate the following into Italian:

1. Does he have any?

2. He doesn't know what to do.

3. He arrived from Rome today.

4. It was done by Maria.

5. Our mother and theirs.

6. How much money does it cost?

7. Whom do you see?

8. This one is good.

9. He has nothing to do.

LEZIONE NONA

LESSON NINE

CAMINO A MILANO

L'Abergatore: *Al telefono.* Buon giorno, signore. Sono le sei e fra cinque minuti vi manderò la prima colazione.

Marco: Buon giorno, e grazie. *A Maria.* È tempo di alzarsi e di cominciare il camino a Milano.

Con le valigie pronte, pagano il conto e, di nuovo in macchina, continuano verso Milano. Ma in via, si fermano a Bologna.

Maria: Che bella città. Bologna ha l'aspetto medioevale.

Marco: Sì, infatti, è una delle più antiche città dell'Italia. Guarda qua, l'Università di Bologna, la più antica d'Europa. La Facoltà di Legge Romana fu stabilita nell'undicesimo secolo. E le facoltà di medicina, di teologia e di arti e scienze, nel quattordicesimo secolo.

Maria: Senti, Marco, è già mezzogiorno ed ho fame. Perchè non ci fermiamo in questa piccola trattoria per rinovore l'energia.

Marco: Una bell'idea. Anche io ho fame. Questo deve essere uno dei ristoranti frequentati dagli studenti.

Entrano e si sedono.

Marco: *Al cameriere.* Spaghetti con salsa bolognese, la pietanza speciale di Bologna, per due. Ma per favore, mi vuol spiegare come si prepara?

Il Cameriere: Ma certo. Con prosciutto, carne di bue tritata, aglio, pomodori, apio, prezzemolo, marsala, e maggiorana.

Marco: Benissimo, e mezza caraffa di vino rosso bolognese.

ON TO MILAN

The Hotelier: *On the telephone.* Good morning, sir. It's six o'clock and I'll be sending up breakfast in five minutes.

Mark: Good morning, and thanks. *To Maria.* It's time to get up and begin our trip to Milan.

With their valises ready, they pay the bill and, again in the car, continue toward Milan. But on the way they stop off at Bologna.

Maria: What a beautiful city. Bologna looks medieval.

Mark: Yes, in fact, it is one of the oldest cities in Italy. Look here, the University of Bologna, the oldest in Europe. The Faculty of Roman Law was established in the eleventh century. And the Faculties of Medicine, of Theology and of Arts and Sciences, in the fourteenth century.

Maria: Look, Mark, it's already noon and I'm hungry. Suppose we stop off at this small restaurant and renew our energy.

Mark: A good idea. I'm hungry, too. This must be one of the restaurants frequented by students.

They enter and are seated.

Marco: *To the waiter.* Spaghetti with Bolognese sauce, Bologna's special dish, for two. But please tell me how it's prepared.

The Waiter: Of course. With *prosciutto*, ground beef, garlic, tomatoes, celery, parsley, Marsala, and marjoram.

Mark: Fine, and half a carafe of Bolognese red wine.

VOCABULARY

aglio	garlic
alzarsi	get up (bed)
anche	too, also
antica -che, f.	ancient, old
apio	celery
arti e science	arts and sciences
aspetto	aspect
bolognese	Bolognese
bue	beef
buon giorno	good morning
caraffa	carafe
carne	meat
casa	house
città	city
colazione, prima	breakfast
continuano	they continue
conto, il	bill, the
deve essere	must be
energia	energy
fa	makes
facoltà	faculty
fame, ho	I am hungry
fermano, si	they stop off
fermiamo, ci	we stop off
fra	within
frequentati	frequented
fu	was
guarda qua	look here
già	already
ha	has
infatti	in fact
legge	law

maggiorana	marjoram
manderò	I shall send
marsala	Marsala wine
medicina	medicine
medioevale	medieval
mezza, f.	half
mezzogiorno	noon
minuti	minutes
nuovo, di	again
pagano	they pay
per favore	please
pietanza	dish
pomodori	tomatoes
prepara, si	is prepared
prezzemolo	parsley
pronte, f., pl.	ready
prosciutto	cured ham
quattordicesimo	fourteenth
rinovare	renew
ristoranti	restaurants
romana, f.	Roman
rosso	red
salsa	sauce
secolo	century
sedono, si	they sit down
senti	listen
sei, sono le	it's six o'clock
signore	sir, mister
speciale	special
spiegare	explain
stabilita, f.	established
storica	historic
studenti, dagli	by the students
telefono	telephone
teologia	theology

tempo	time
trattor*i*a	restaurant, inn
tritata, *f.*	ground, chopped
undic*e*simo	eleventh
università	university
val*i*gie	valises, suitcases
verso	toward
via, in	on the way
vino	wine
vuol (e)	wish, will

LOCUZIONI — EXPRESSIONS

buon giorno	good morning
fra cinque minuti	in five minutes
la prima colazione	breakfast
è tempo di alzarsi	it's time to get up
di nuovo	again
in via	on the way
si fermano	they stop
ha l'aspetto medioevale	looks medieval
in fatti	in fact
la più antica città	the oldest city
guarda qua	look here
la facoltà di medicina	the school of medicine
è già mezzogiorno	it's already noon
ho fame	I'm hungry
per rinovare l'energia	to renew our energy
una bell'idea	a good idea
frequentato dagli studenti	frequented by the students
salsa bolognese	Bolognese sauce
la pietanza speciale	the special dish
per favore	please
mi vuol spiegare ?	will you please explain?
ma certo	of course
prosciutto	cured ham
carne di bue tritata	ground beef
aglio	garlic
pomodori	tomatoes
mezza caraffa	half a carafe

ESERCIZI — EXERCISES:

1. Copy the text, read it aloud and translate it.

2. Make up sentences with the following phrases and repeat them three times:
   è già mezzogiorno; ho fame; mi vuol spiegare; è tempo di alzarsi; buon giorno.

3. Translate into Italian:
   established in the eleventh century; it's six o'clock; the oldest city; half a carafe; it's already noon.

4. Translate into English:
   mi vuol spiegare; ha l'aspetto medioevale; carne di bue tritata; è tempo di alzarsi.

5. Memorize:
   fra cinque minuti vi manderò la prima colazione; ha l'aspetto medioevale; la facoltà di medicina; di nuovo; salsa bolognese; una bell'idea.

GRAMMAR

IX. ADVERBS

Adverbs do not agree with nouns, adjectives, or verbs.
They are invariable.

There are two types of adverbs: *conjunctive* and *disjunctive*.

Conjunctive adverbs are so-called because they stand next to, and precede the verb (**con** -*with*).

1. **ci** (*there*)

    (a) indicating place:

    Va a Roma? No, non **ci** va.   *Is he going to Rome? No, he's*
                                      not going.
    (Note: **vi** (*there*) is rarely used.)

    (b) used emphatically at the beginning of a phrase:

    C'era una volta.   *Once upon a time.*

2. **ne** (*of it*, etc.) An unemphatic adverbial pronoun referring to a prepositional phrase introduced by **di**.

    Ha parlato <u>di suo padre</u>?   *Has he spoken of his father?*
    Sì, **ne** ha parlato.   *Yes, he has spoken of him.*

Disjunctive adverbs are so-called because they do not receive the action of the verb; as it were, they are *dis*-joined from it. There are four groups of disjunctives: *of place*; *of time*; *of quantity*; and *of manner*.

1. Adverbs of Place

qui or qua, *here,* near the speaker
costì or costà, *there,* near the person addressed
lì or là, *over there,* away from both
vicino, *nearby, close*
lontano, *distant, far*

Dove è? È **qua.**	*Where is it? It's here.*
Che fai **costà?**	*What are you doing there?*
Lo vedo **là.**	*I see him over there.*
La sua casa è **vicino.**	*His house is nearby.*
La cttà è **lontano.**	*The city is far away.*

2. Adverbs of Time

avantieri, *day before yesterday*	**ora,** *now*
domane, *tomorrow*	**ora ora,** *right away*
dopo domane, *day after tomorrow*	**presto,** *soon*
fa, *ago*	**sempre,** *always*
ieri, *yesterday*	**spesso,** *often*
ierisera, *last night*	**stamane,** *this morning*
non...mai, *never*	**stanotte,** *last night*
oggi, *today*	**stasera,** *this evening*

Non ti ha **mai** parlato.	*He has never spoken to you.*
Lo faccio **ora ora.**	*I'll do it right away.*
Tre anni **fa.**	*Three years ago.*
Arrivò **ierisera.**	*He arrived last night.*
Ci vado **dopo domane.**	*I'll go the day after tomorrow.*
Lui è **sempre** manso.	*He is always well behaved.*

3. Adverbs of Quantity

assai, *a lot, much, enough*   **tanto**, *much, so much*
troppo, *too much, too*   **poco**, *little, small, few*
tutto, *all, whole, entire*

Ti vuole bene **assai**.   *He is very fond of you.*
Sono **troppo** stanco.   *I am too tired.*

4. Adverbs of Manner

(a) Adverbs of manner are formed by adding the suffix **-mente** to the feminine form of the adjective. (Adverbs of manner answer the question: How is it done?)

chiaro, -a, *clear*   **chiaramente,** *clearly*
franco, -a, *frank*   **francamente,** *frankly*

(b) *So* meaning *it* is translated as **lo**.

Lo faccio.   *I do so.*
Lo crede.   *He thinks so.*
Lo dicono.   *They say so.*

Comparison

Adverbs are compared like adjectives.

1. Regular:
   grande, *large*; **più grande,** *larger*; **il più grande,** *the largest*
   piccolo, *small*; **più piccolo,** *smaller*; **il più piccolo,** *the smallest*

2. Irregular:
    bene, *well;* **meglio,** *better;* **il meglio,** *the best*
    male, *bad;* **peggio,** *worse;* **il peggio,** *the worst*

sì, no, come

Yes is **sì.** *No* is **no.** *What* meaning *what do you say?* is **come. Che** is often used to introduce questions.

Perchè non rispondi? **Come? Che** sei sordo?
Why don't you answer? What? Are you deaf?

ESERCIZI — EXERCISES:

Translate the following into Italian:

1. His house is far.

2. He doesn't have any.

3. I can't see too well.

4. I'll go this evening.

5. Paul is bigger than Mark.

6. She is always good.

7. Four years ago.

8. What? Are you deaf?

9. He never speaks to me.

10. He'll go there tomorrow.

LEZIONE DECIMA

LESSON TEN

MILANO

Marco e Maria sono arrivati a Milano, dove sono andati a trovare i nuovi amici, Gianni e Anna Orlando.

Marco: Che piacere di ritrovarvi.

Maria: Un vero piacere.

Gianni: Siete benvenuti.

Anna: Dopo di riposarvi, vi vogliamo far fare un giro della nostra città, che è il centro economico dell'Italia...

Gianni: E il centro della moda di Europa. Vi vogliamo mostrare *l'ultima cena di Cristo* di Leonardo da Vinci, nella chiesa di Santa Maria delle Grazie.

Anna: E la famosa Scala di Milano, il più famoso teatro dell'opera del mondo, dove Giuseppe Verdi ebbe i suoi più grandi trionfi.

Gianni: E non dobbiamo dimenticare la casa dove Alessandro Manzoni scrisse *I Promessi Sposi*.

Finalmente quando avranno quasi terminato il giro, arrivano al Duomo.

Anna: Al mio parere, il Duomo è il più importante monumento di Milano. È la più grande cattedrale gotica del mondo. Hanno cominciato a fabbricarla nel 1386 e l' hanno finito cinque secoli più tardi.

Marco: Stupendo!

Maria: C'è tanto da vedere in Italia. Peccato che domane dobbiamo tornar in casa! Ma vi giuro che torneremo.

MILAN

Mark and Maria have arrived in Milan, where they have looked up their friends, Gianni and Anna Orlando.

Mark: What a pleasure to see you again.

Maria: A real pleasure.

Gianni: Welcome.

Anna: After you've rested, we want to have you tour our city, which is the economic center of Italy.

Gianni: And Europe's style center. We want to show you Leonardo da Vinci's *Last Supper,* in the Santa Maria delle Grazie church.

Anna: And the famous Scala di Milan, the most famous opera house in the world, where Giuseppe Verdi had his greatest triumphs.

Gianni: And we mustn't forget the house where Alessandro Manzoni wrote *The Betrothed.*

Finally, when they have almost finished the tour they arrive at the Duomo.

Anna: In my opinion, the Duomo is Milan's most important monument. It is the largest Gothic cathedral in the world. They began building it in 1386 and finished it five centuries later.

Mark: Marvelous!

Maria: There is so much to see in Italy. It's a shame that tomorrow we'll have to return home. But I swear that we shall return.

VOCABULARY

arrívano	they arrive
arrivati, sono	they arrived
avranno	have, shall
benvenuti, *pl.*	welcome
casa, in	home
cattedrale	cathedral
cena	supper
centro	center
chiesa	church
città	city
Cristo	Christ
dico	I say
dobbiamo	we must
domane	tomorrow
dove	where
ebbe	he had
econ*o*mico	economic
Europa	Europe
fabbricare	to build
famosa, *f.*	famous
far fare	to have to do
finalmente	finally
finito	finished
giuro, vi	swear, to you
g*o*tica, *f.*	Gothic
hanno cominciato	they began
mondo	world
monumento	monument
mostrare	to show
*o*pera	opera
parere	opinion
peccato	pity, shame, sin

piacere, che	pleasure, what a
quando	when
quasi	almost
riposarvi	rest yourselves
santa, *f.*	saint
*s*ecoli	centuries
siete	you are
stupendo!	marvelous!
tanto	so much
tardi, più	later
teatro	theater
terminato	finished
testa	head
torneremo	we shall return
trionfi	triumphs
trovare	to find
tornar (e)	return
*u*ltima, *f.*	the last
vedere, da	to see
vero	real
visitare	to visit
vogliamo	we want

LOCUZIONI — EXPRESSIONS

piacere di ritrovarvi	a pleasure to see you again
un vero piacere	a real pleasure
siete benvenuti	you're welcome
dopo di riposarvi	after resting
vi vogliamo far fare	we want you to do
il centro economico dell'Italia	Italy's economic center
il centro della moda di Europa	Europe's style center
l'ultima cena di Cristo	Christ's Last Supper
il più famoso teatro	the most famous theater
i suoi più grandi trionfi	his greatest triumphs
non dobbiamo dimenticare	we mustn't forget
I Promessi Sposi	*The Betrothed*
al mio parere	in my opinion
il più importante monumento	the most important monument
la più grande cattedrale gotica	the largest Gothic cathedral
del mondo	in the world
hanno cominciato a fabbricarla	they began to build it
cinque secoli più tardi	five centuries later
stupendo!	marvelous!
c'è tanto da vedere in Italia	there's so much to see in Italy
peccato che	a shame that
dobbiamo tornar in casa	we have to return home
vi giuro che torneremo	I swear we shall return

ESERCIZI — EXERCISES:

1. Copy the text, read it aloud and translate it.

2. Make up sentences with the following phrases and repeat them
   three times:
   il centro economico dell'Italia; vi giuro che torneremo; al mio
   parere; l'ultima cena di Cristo; un vero piacere.

3. Translate into Italian:
   his greatest triumphs; Europe's style center; a pleasure to see you
   again; *The Betrothed*; I swear we shall return.

4. Translate into English:
   vi vogliamo far fare un giro della nostra città; c'è tanto da vedere
   in Italia; peccato che dobbiamo tornar in casa; al mio parere.

5. Memorize:
   peccato che dobbiamo tornar in casa; c'è tanto da vedere in Italia;
   vi giuro che torneremo; l'ultima cena di Cristo; la più grande
   catttedrale gotica; i suoi più grandi trionfi.

GRAMMAR

X. THE VERB SYSTEM

Italian has three conjugations: I - **are**; II - **ere**; III - **ire**.

See the Appendix for conjugation of the irregular verbs. This section offers a simplified and reduced version and does not include some of the less frequently used tenses, such as the *imperfect subjunctive*.

Auxiliary Verbs

Italian has two auxiliary verbs, *avere* (to have) and *essere* (to be). The regular endings in the verbs that follow are indicated here by a hyphen (-) after the stem.

av-ere, *to have*

Infinitive	Present participle	Past participle
av-ere	av-endo	av-uto

Present Indicative		Imperfect		Preterite	
I have, etc.		*I had, was having, etc.*		*I had, etc.*	
ho	abbiamo	av-evo	av-evamo	ebbi	av-emmo
hai	av-ete	av-evi	av-evate	av-esti	av-este
ha	hanno	av-eva	av-evano	ebbe	ebbero

Imperative

abbi *have* (you, sg.)
abbiate *have* (you, pl.)
abbiamo *let us have*

Future
I shall have, etc.

av-rò	av-remo
av-rai	av-rete
av-rà	av-ranno

Conditional
I should (would) have, etc.

av-rei	av-remmo
av-resti	av-reste
av-rebbe	av-rebbero

Present Perfect
I have had, etc.

ho av-uto	abbiamo av-uto
hai av-uto	avete av-uto
ha av-uto	hanno av-uto

Present Subjunctive
I may have, etc.

abbia	abbiamo
abbia	abbiate
abbia	abbiano

ess-ere, *to be*

Infinitive	Present participle	Past participle
ess-ere	ess-endo	stato

Present Indicative		Imperfect		Preterite	
I am, etc.		*I was, used to be, etc.*		*I was, etc.*	
sono	siamo	ero	eravamo	fui	fummo
sei	siete	eri	eravate	fosti	foste
è	sono	era	erano	fu	furono

Imperative
sii *be* (you, s.)
siate *be* (you, pl.)
siamo *let us be*

<table>
<tr><td>

Future
I shall be, etc.

sarò	saremo
sarai	sarete
sarà`	saranno

</td><td>

Conditional
I should (would) be, etc.

sarei	saremmo
saresti	sareste
sarebbe	sarebbero

</td></tr>
<tr><td>

Present Perfect
I have been, etc.

sono stato	siamo stati
sei stato	siete stati
è stato	sono stati

</td><td>

Present Subjunctive
I may be, etc.

sia	siamo
sia	siate
sia	siano

</td></tr>
</table>

THE REGULAR VERBS

First Conjugation -are

parl-are, *to speak*

Infinitive	Present participle	Past participle
parl-are	parl-ando	parl-ato

Present Indicative		Imperfect		Preterite	
I speak, etc.		*I used to speak, etc.*		*I spoke, etc.*	
parl-o	parl-iamo	parl-avo	parl-avamo	parl-ai	parl-ammo
parl-i	parl-ate	parl-avi	parl-avate	parl-asti	parl-aste
parl-a	parl-ano	parl-ava	parl-avano	parl-ò	par-larono

Imperative

Positive:
parla *speak* (you, s.)
parlate *speak* (you, pl.)
parliamo *let us speak*

Negative:
non parlare *do not speak* (s.)
non parlate *do not speak* (pl.)
non parliamo *let us not speak*

Future		Conditional	
I shall be, etc.		*I should (would) be, etc.*	
parl-erò	parl-eremo	parl-erei	parl-eremmo
parl-erai	parl-erete	parl-eresti	parl-ereste
parl-erà	parl-eranno	parl-erebbe	parl-erebbero

Present Perfect		Present Subjunctive	
I have spoken, etc.		*I may speak, etc.*	
ho parl-ato	abbiamo parl-ato	parl-i	parl-iamo
hai parl-ato	avete parl-ato	parl-i	parl-iate
ha parl-ato	hanno parl-ato	parl-i	parl-ino

Second Conjugation - ere

This conjugation includes verbs whose infinitives have the stress on the third syllable from the end — the antipenult.

vend-ere, *to sell*

Infinitive	Present participle	Past participle
vend-ere	vend-endo	vend-uto

Present Indicative — *I sell, etc.*
Imperfect — *I used to sell, etc.*
Preterite — *I sold, etc.*

vend-o	vend-iamo	vend-evo	vend-evamo	vend-ei	vend-emmo
vend-i	vend-ete	vend-e vi	vend-evate	vend-esti	vend-este
vend-e	vend-ono	vend-eva	vend-evano	vend-è	vend-erono

Imperative
Positive:
vend-i *sell* (you, s.)
vend-ete *sell* (you, pl.)
vend-iamo *let us sell*

Negative:
non vendere *do not sell* (s.)
non vendete *do not sell* (pl.)
non vendiamo *let us not sell*

Future
I shall be, etc.

vender-ò	vender-emo
vender-ai	vender-ete
vender-à	vender-anno

Conditional
I should (would) be, etc.

vender-ei	vender-emmo
vender-esti	vender-este
vender-ebbe	vender-ebbero

Present Perfect
I have sold, etc.

ho vend-uto	abbiamo vend-uto
hai vend-uto	avete vend-uto
ha vend-uto	hanno vend-uto

Present Subjunctive
I may sell, etc.

vend-a	vend-iamo
vend-a	vend-iate
vend-a	vend-ano

Third Conjugation - ire

part-ire, *to leave, depart*

Infinitive	Present participle	Past participle
part-ire	part-endo	par-tito

Present Indicative
I depart, etc.

Imperfect
I used to depart, etc.

Preterite
I departed, etc.

part-o	part-iamo	part-ivo	part-iv*a*mo	part-*i*i	part-immo
part-i	part-ite	part-ivi	par-iv*a*te	part-isti	part-iste
part-e	p*a*rt-ono	part-iva	part-*i*vano	part-ì	part-*i*rono

Imperative

Positive:
parti *leave* (you, s.)
partite *leave* (you, pl.)
partiamo *let us leave*

Negative:
non partire *do not leave* (s.)
non partite *do not leave* (pl.)
non partiamo *let us not leave*

Future
I shall leave, etc.

partir-ò	partir-emo
partir-ai	partir-ete
partir-à	partir-anno

Conditional
I should (would) leave, etc.

partir-ei	partir-emmo
partir-esti	partir-este
partir-*e*bbe	partir-*e*bbero

Present Perfect
I have left, etc.

sono part-ito	siamo part-iti
sei part-ito	siete part-iti
è part-ito	sono part-iti

Present Subjunctive
I may leave, etc.

part-a	part-iamo
part-a	part-iate
part-a	p*a*rt-ano

finire, *to finish*

The third conjugation has a number of verbs whose stem changes in the first, second and third persons singular, in the third person plural of the present indicative, and in the second person singular of the positive imperative. Like **finire**, these are:

capire, *to understand*	**preferire**, *to prefer*
costruire, *to build*	**pulire**, *to clean, polish*
guarire, *to get well*	**restituire**, *to give back*
obbedire, *to obey*	**spedire**, *to mail (a package)*

Finire is conjugated as follows:

Present Indicative

fini-sco	fin-iamo
fini-sci	fin-ite
fin-isce	fin-*i*scono

Present Subjunctive

fini-sca	fin-iamo
fini-sca	fin-iate
fini-sca	fin*i*-scano

Imperative

fin-isci *finish* (you, s.)
fin-ite *finish* (you, pl.)
fin-iamo *let us finish*

IRREGULAR VERBS
(See the Appendix for a complete treatment)

Note the following uses of verbs:

1. When used as the subject or direct object of a verb, the English gerund (ending in -ing) is rendered in Italian by the *infinitive*.

Mi piace <u>viaggiare</u>.	*I like traveling.*
Odio <u>studiare</u>.	*I hate studying.*

2. The English gerund preceded by a preposition (and followed by an infinitive) is translated as follows:

di, *of* — **invece di**, *instead of* — **senza**, *without* — **dopo di**, *after* — **prima di**, *before*

Il vizio **di** <u>fumare</u>.	*The habit of <u>smoking</u>.*
Dopo di <u>parlare</u>...	*After <u>speaking</u>...*
Invece di <u>criticare</u>...	*Instead of <u>criticizing</u>...*
Prima di <u>morire</u>...	*Before <u>dying</u>...*
Parlano **senza** <u>pensare</u>.	*They speak **without** <u>thinking</u>.*

3. After the verbs **fare**, *to make* or *to have (i.e. to cause)*, **sentire**, *to hear*, and **vedere**, *to see*, Italian uses the infinitive to express the English past participle.

Si fa **capire**.	*He makes himself <u>understood</u>.*
Faccio **fare** un paio di scarpe.	*I'm having a pair of shoes <u>made</u>.*
Sento **dire**...	*I hear it <u>said</u>...*

4. After the verb **lasciare**, *to let,* and often after the preposition **da**, an active infinitive is used to translate a passive one in English.

Si lascia **ingannare**.   *He is letting himself be deceived.*
Non c'è niente da **fare**.   *There is nothing to be done.*

5. When used as an adjective, the past participle is inflected like any other adjective.

Questi vasi sono **rotti**.   *These vases are broken.*

6. In negative commands, the infinitive is always used instead of the second person singular of the imperative.

F*a*llo. *Do it.*   Non lo **fare**. *Don't do it.*

7. The imperfect dènotes a continuing action, while the preterite is used to describe an action that has been completed.

Entrò mentre **dorm*i*vano**.   *He entered while they were sleeping.*
Lo **fece** l'anno passato.   *He did it last year.*

ESERCIZI — EXERCISES:

A. Conjugate (a) **parlare**, *I speak, you speak, etc.* (b) **vendere** and (c) **partire** in the present indicative.

B. Translate the following into Italian:

1. I am afraid.

2. Do it today.

3. I make myself understood.

4. I hear it said that he speaks well.

5. I like studying.

6. I'll finish it tomorrow.

7. Instead of criticizing, do it.

8. Don't let yourself be deceived.

9. He makes himself understood.

10. He speaks without thinking.

KEY TO EXERCISES

LESSON 1

2. Dove possiamo prendere un tassì? Tutti chiamano questo aeroporto Fiumicino. Hai prenotato una camera per due?

3. Now we must present our passports. You may pass. At customs. The officer.

Grammar Section

1. Marco Martini è un buon medico.
2. Maria Martini è professore d'inglese.
3. Gianni è un buon poeta.

LESSON 2

3. Permettetimi di presentarmi. Siamo nati in America. Mille grazie. Voi siete Italiani?

4. Here is my telephone number. We have visited relatives in America. Come and spend one or two days with us. Happy to meet you.

Grammar Section

1. Un paio di uova.
2. Marco e Gianni sono amici.
3. Centinaia di miglie.
4. I medici non sono Italiani; sono Greci.
5. I fratelli sono colleghi.

LESSON 3

3. Il nostro letto è comodo. Voglio provare il bar qua vicino. Oggi il giro è a piedi. Io preferisco lavarmi nella vasca da bagno.

4. Don't you think it's a reasonable price? I prefer bathing in a bathtub. I prefer a shower. Well then let's do that.

Grammar Section

l. Paolo è il fratello maggiore.
2. Nino è più piccolo di Paolo.
3. Questa stanza è la più grande.

LESSON 4

3. ma certo, sono d'accordo; il cappuccino è delizioso; spettacoli crudeli; se ti vesti in una toga; qua vicino.

4. freshly-squeezed orange juice; we must ask for directions; can you tell me?

Grammar Section

1. Un boccone di cappuccino.
2. La stanza è molto larga.
3. Giannino è il fratello di Maria.

Lesson 5

3. andiamo; vogliamo mangiare una pietanza romana; vi raccomando una pietanza speciale romana; il cameriere da loro la lista

4. we are both hungry; a tip for the waiter; what do you recommend?; a table for two

Grammar Section

1. Una trentina di case.
2. Due paia di scarpe.
3. Maria ha due dozzine di libri.
4. Sono le quattro e mezzo.
5. Sei di maggio.
6. Duemila cento.

Lesson 6

3. Marco, tu sempre che scherzi; quando posso venire per un' ondulazione permanente?; mi sta bene; escono dal negozio

4. a stylish dress; may I try it on?; a beauty parlor; a bottle of mouthwash

Grammar Section

1. Ci vestiamo.
2. Lo fa per me.
3. Dammelo.
4. Non lo voglio.
5. Veli da.
6. Ne volete?
7. Carlo mi da il libro.
8. Si veste.
9. Parlano.

LESSON 7

3. è un poco caro; trippa fiorentina per due; il piatto del giorno; dopo tre ore di viaggio; non ti pare?

4. This is a fine car; it's worthwhile; today's special dish; a fine room with two beds; it's already noon.

Grammar Section

1. Nostra figlia è bella.
2. Questo libro è suo.
3. L'uomo a chi parlo.
4. Chi parla?
5. Quella donna è bella.
6. Nostra madre e a la sua.
7. Quanti soldi costa?
8. A chi vedi?
9. Questo è buono.

LESSON 8

3. giganti del Rinascimento; davvero troppo; non ne posso più; una buona idea; non ti pare?

4. what treasures!; I can't take anymore; really too much; look; the famous Florentine steaks.

Grammar Section

1. Ne ha?
2. Non sa che fare.
3. Arrivò da Roma oggi.
4. Fu fatto da Maria.

5. Nostra madre e la loro.
6. Quanto costa?
7. A chi vedi?
8. Questo è buono.
9. Non ha niente da fare.

LESSON 9

3. fu stabilita nell'undicesimo secolo; sono le sei; la più antica città; mezza caraffa; è già mezzogiorno.

4. will you explain to me; it looks medieval; ground beef; it's time to get up.

Grammar Section

1. Sua casa è lontano.
2. Non ne ha.
3. Non posso vedere troppo bene.
4. Ci andrò stasera.
5. Paolo è più grande di Marco.
6. Lei è sempre buona.
7. Quattro anni fa.
8. Come? Che sei sordo?
9. Non mi parla mai.
10. Ci andrà domane.

LESSON 10

3. i suoi più grandi trionfi; il centro della moda di Europa; piacere di rivedervi; *I Promessi Sposi*; vi giuro che torneremo.

4. we want to have you tour our city; there is so much to see in Italy; it's a shame that we'll have to return home; in my opinion.

Grammar Section

B. 1. Ho paura.
    2. Fallo oggi.
    3. Mi faccio capire.
    4. Sento dire che parla bene.
    5. Mi piace studiare.
    6. Lo finirò domane.
    7. Invece di criticare, fallo.
    8. Non ti lasciare ingannare.
    9. Si fa capire.
    10. Parla senza pensare.

APPENDIX

THE IRREGULAR VERBS

First Conjugation -are

The following irregular verbs belong to the first conjugation:
dare, fare, stare. The irregular forms (paradigms) are underlined.

dare, *to give*
Pres. Ind.:	do, dai, da, diamo, date, danno
Preterite:	detti, dasti, dette, demmo, deste, dettero

fare, *to do*
Present participle:	facendo
Pres. Ind.:	fo or faccio, fai, fa, facciamo, fate, fanno
Imperfect:	facevo, facevi, etc...
Preterite:	feci, facesti, fece, facemmo, faceste, fecero

stare, *to stay, to be, to remain*
Pres. Ind.:	sto, stai, sta, stiamo, state, stanno
Preterite:	stetti, stesti, stette, stemmo, steste, stettero

Second Conjugation - ere

The following are among the most common irregular verbs. Consult a dictionary for those not listed here. The irregular paradigms are underlined.

cadere, *to fall*
Preterite: caddi, cadesti, cadde, cademmo, cadeste, caddero

dovere, *to be obliged to*
Pres. Ind.:   devo, devi, deve, dobbiamo, dovete, devono

mettere, *to put, to place*
Past Part.:   messo
Preterite: misi, mettesti, mise, mettemmo, metteste, misero

nascere, *to be born*
Past Part.:   nato
Pres. Ind.:   nasco, nasci, nasce, nasciamo, nascete, nascono
Preterite: nacqui, nascesti, nacque, nascemmo, nasceste,
                     nacquero

potere, *to be able to*
Pres. Ind.:   posso, puoi, può, possiamo, potete, possono

sapere, *to know*
Pres. Ind.:   so, sai, sa, sappiamo, sapete, sanno
Preterite: seppi, sapesti, seppe, sapemmo, sapeste, seppero

tenere, *to hold*
Pres. Ind.:   tengo, tieni, tiene, teniamo, tenete, tengono
Preterite: tenni, tenesti, tenne, tenemmo, teneste, tennero
Future: terrò, terrai, terrà, terremo, terrete, terranno

valere, *to be worth*
Pres. Ind.:   valgo, vali, vale, valiamo, valete, valgono
Preterite: valsi, valesti, valse, valemmo, valeste, valsero
Future: varrò, varrai, varrà, varremo, varrete, varranno

vedere, *to see*
Preterite: vidi, vedesti, vide, vedemmo, vedeste, videro

volere, *to be willing, to want*
Pres. Ind.:   voglio, vuoi, vuole, vogliamo, volete, vogliono
Preterite: volli, volesti, volle, volemmo, voleste, vollero

Third Conjugation - ire

aprire, *to open*
Past Part.:   aperto

dire, *to say*
Pres. Part.:   dicendo
Past Part.:   detto
Pres. Ind.:   dico, dici, dice, diciamo, dite, dicono
Preterite: dissi, dicesti, disse, dicemmo, diceste, dissero

morire, *to die*
Pres. Ind.:   muoio, muori, muore, moriamo, morite, muoiono
Future: morrò, morrai, morrà, morremo, morrete,
                    morranno

salire, *to go forth*
Pres. Ind.:   salgo, sali, sale, saliamo, salite, salgono

udire, *to hear*
Pres. Ind.:   odo, odi, ode, udiamo, udite, odono

uscire, *to go out*
Pres. Ind.:   esco, esci, esce, usciamo, uscite, escono

venire, *to come*
Pres. Ind.:   vengo, vieni, viene, veniamo, venite, vengono
Preterite: venni, veniste, venne, venimmo, veniste, vennero
Future: verrò, verrai, verrà, verremo, verrete, verranno

I TALIAN-E NGLISH
V OCABULARY

A

a, *prep.*, to, at

abbiamo, *1st pl., pres. ind.,*
avere, to have

accordo, d', *n. m.,* agreed

acqua, *n. f.,* water; — dentifricia, mouthwash

adesso, *adv.,* now

addio, *interjection,* good-bye

aeroporto, *n. m.,* airport

affinchè, *conj.,* in order that

aglio, *n. m.,* garlic

al, to the

albergatore, *n. m.,* hotelier

albergo, *n. m.,* hotel

alcuno, *adj.,* some

allora, *adv.,* then

altro, -a, *pron.,* other

alzarsi, *vb.,* to get up (bed)

amico, *n. m.,* friend

anche, *conj.,* also, too

andate, *2nd pl. pres. ind.,*
andare, to go

andiamo, *1st pl., pres. ind.,*
andare, to go

animale, -i, *n. m.,* animal, -s

anno, *n. m.,* year

antico, *adj.,* old, ancient

anzi, *conj.,* rather

apio, *n. m.,* celery

araldo, *n. m.,* herald

aranci, *n. m.,* oranges

arriviamo, *1st pl., pres. ind.,*
arrivare, to arrive

arrivano, *3d pl., pres. ind.,*
arrivare, to arrive

arrivata, *n. f.,* arrival

arrivati, sono, *3d pl., pres. perf.,*
arrivare; they have arrived

arrivò, *3d s. pret.,* arrivare, to
arrive

arte, *n. f.,* art

artista, -i, *n. m.,* artist, -s

aspetto, *n. m.,* aspect

aspirina, *n. f.,* aspirin

assai, *adv.,* a lot

attimo, *n. m.,* instant

autobiografia, *n. f.*
autobiography

autobus, *n. m.,* bus

autostrada, *n. f.,* road, highway

avanti, *adv., prep.,* forward!

avere, *vb.,* to have

avete, *2nd pl., pres. ind.,* avere,
to have

autista, *n. m.,* driver

B

bagno, *n. m.,* bath

bar, *n. m.,* coffee shop

basta, *3d s., pres. ind.,* bastare,
to be enough

bellissimo, *adj.,* very beautiful

bello, *adj.,* beautiful

bene, *adv.,* well

benissimo, *adv.,* very good

benvenuto, *pron.,* welcome

benzina, *n. f.*, gasoline
bicchiere, *n. m.*, glass
bisogno, *n. m.*, need
bisogna, *3d s., pres. ind.,*
    bisognare to be necessary
bistecca, -che, *n. f.*, beefsteak, -s
blu, *adj.*, blue
bocca, *n. f.*, mouth
bolognese, *adj.*, Bolognese
bottega, -ghe, *n. f.*, shop, -s
bottiglia, *n. f.*, bottle
bue, *n. m., (pl.* buoi), ox, beef
buono, *adj., m.*, good
burro, *n. m.*, butter

C

caffè, *n. m.*, coffee
camera, *n. f.*, room
cameriere, *n. m.*, waiter
camino (in), *n. m.*, road (on the)
capisco, *1st s., pres. ind.,* capire,
    to understand
capitale, *n. f.*, capital
cappuccino, *n. m.*, cappuccino
caraffa, *n. f.*, carafe
carne, *n. f.*, meat
caro, *adj.*, dear, expensive
carta stradale, *n. f.*, street map
casa, (in) *n. f.*, home (at)
cassiere, *n. m.*, cashier
cattedrale, *n. f.*, cathedral
c'è, *3d sing.*, essere, to be; there is
cena, *n. f.*, dinner

centinaia, *n. m.*, about hundred
centro, *n. m.*, center
c'erano, *3d pl., imperf.*, essere,
    to be; there were
certo, ma, *adv.*, of course
che, *rel. pron.*, that
chi, *rel. pron.*, who, which
chiama, *3d s., pres. ind.,*
    chiamare, to call
chiamano, *3d pl., pres. ind.,*
    chiamare, to call
chiamare, *vb.*, to call
chiamata, *n. f.*, call
chiamate (vi), *2nd pl., pres. ind.,*
    chiamare, call (me)
chiamo, *1st s., pres. ind.,*
    chiamare, to call; mi chiamo,
    my name is
chiesa, *n. f.*, church
ci, *pron.*, us, to us
ci, *adv.*, there
cinque, *adj.*, five
città, *n. f.*, city
colazione, prima, *n. f.*, breakfast
colera, *n. m.*, cholera
collega, *n. m.*, colleague
come, *adv.*, how, like, *conj.*, as
    come? *adv.*, what?
cominciare, *vb.*, to begin
cominciato, *p. part.,*
    cominciare, *to begin*
commissa, *n. f.*, saleslady
comodo, *adj.*, comfortable
con, *prep.*, with
conoscere, *vb.*, to know

conserva di frutta, *n. f.*, fruit preserves

Consolato Italiano, *n. m.*, Italian Consulate

contento, *adj.*, content, happy

continu*a*mo, *1st pl., pres. ind.*, continu*a*re, to continue; cont*i*nuano, *3d pl., pres. ind.*

continu*a*re, *vb.*, to continue

conto, *n. m.*, bill

contra, *prep.*, against

coppia, -e, *n. f.*, couple, -s

cornetto, *n. m.*, filled croissant

corto, *adj.*, short

cosa, *n. f.*, thing

così, *adv.*, thus, so, just that

così bene, *adv. phr.* so well

costa, *3d s., pres. ind.*, costare, to cost

crema, *n. f.*, cream, — per la barba, shaving cream

Cristo, *n. m.*, Christ

criticare, *vb.*, to criticize

crudele, -i, *n. m.*, cruel

culturale, *adj.* cultural

D

da, *prep.*, from

danno, *3d pl., pres. ind.*, dare, to give

dare, *vb.*, to give

davvero, *adv.*, indeed, really

delizioso, *adj.*, delicious

dente, *n. m.*, tooth, al dente, firm to the bite (pasta)

destra, *adv.*, right (side)

dette, *3d s., pret.*, dare, to give

di, *prep.*, of

dico, *1st s. pres. ind.*, dire, to say

d*i*cono, *3d pl., pres. ind.*, dire, to say

diecina, *n. f.*, about ten

Dio, *n. m.*, God

differente, *adj.*, different

dimmi, tell me, *2nd s., imp.*, dire, to say, tell

dire, *vb.*, to say, to tell

direi, *1st s., cond.*, dire, to say, to tell

direttamente, *adv.*, directly

direzione, -i, *n. m.*

discreto, *adj.*, modest, reasonable

disse, *3d s., pret.*, dire, to tell

dobbiamo, *3d pl., pres. ind.*, dovere, to have to

doccia, *n. f.*, shower

dogana, *n. f.*, customs

d*o*llaro, *n. m.*, dollar

domand*a*i, *1st s., pret.*, domandare, to ask (for)

dom*a*ndano, *3d pl., pres. ind.*, domandare, to ask (for)

domandare, *vb.*, to ask (for)

domane, *adv.*, tomorrow

dopo, *prep.*, after

dove, *adv.*, where

dozzina, *n. m.*, dozen

due, *adj.*, two
dunque, *adv.*, (so) then

E

e, ed, *conj.*, and
è, *3d s., pres. ind.*, essere, to be
ecco, *adv.*, here is, are; eccoci,
  here we are
economico, *adj.*, economic
elegante, *n. m.*, stylish
energia, *n. f.*, energy
entrano, *3d pl., pres. ind.*,
  entrare, to enter
è proprio così, *adv. phr.*, that's
  right
escono, *3d pl., pres. ind.*, uscire,
  to leave
essere, *vb.*, to be
Europa, *n. f.*, Europe

F

fa, *adv*, ago; *3d s., pres. ind.*,
  fare, to do
fabbricare, *vb.*, to build
facciamo, *1st, pl., pres. ind.*,
  fare, to do
facile, *adj.*, easy
facoltà, *n. f.*, faculty
fame, *n. m.*, hungry, hunger;
  aver(e) fame, to be hungry
famoso, *adj.*, famous

fanno, *3d pl., pres. ind.*, fare, to do
fare, *vb.*, to do; far fare, to have
  to do
farmacia, *n. f.*, drugstore
farmacista, *n.m.*, pharmacist
fatto, *n. m.*, fact
favore, *n. m.*, favor; per —, please
fermarsi, *vb.*, to stop off at
fettuccine, *n. f.*, a wide pasta
figlio, -i, *n. m.*, son, -s
fino, *prep.*, as far as
finalmente, *adv.*, finally
finito, *p. part.*, finire, to finish;
  adj. finished
fiorentino, *adj.*, Florentine
Firenze, *n. m.*, Florence
formaggio, *n. m.*, cheese
foro, *n. m.*, the Forum
forse, *adv.*, perhaps
fra, *prep.*, among, between, within
francese, *n. m., adj., pron.*, French
frascati, *n. m.*, a Roman wine
frequentato, *p. part.*,
  frequentare, to frequent
fresco, -a, *adj.*, fresh
fu, *3d s. pret.*, essere, to be
  fummo, *1st pl., pret.*
fuga, *n. f.*, flight

G

gerente, *n. m.*, manager
già, *adv.*, already
gigante, -i, *n. m.*, giant, -s

giorno, *n. m.*, day
girar(e), *vb.*, to tour
giro, *n. m.*, tour
giuro, *1st s., pres. ind.*, **giurare**,
  to swear
giusto, *adj.*, just right
gladiatore, *n. m.*, gladiator
gotico, *adj.*, Gothic
gran(de), *adj.*, big, great
grazie, *inter.*, thanks; **mille —**,
  many thanks
greco, *n. m.*, Greek
guancia, *n. f.*, cheek
guarda, *s. imp.*, **guardare**, to look
guida, (**patente di**), *n. m.*,
  driver's (license)

H

ha, *3d s., pres. ind.*, **avere**, to
  have; **hai**, *2nd s., pres. ind.*;
  hanno, *3d pl., pres. ind.*

I

ieri, *adv.*, yesterday
idea, *n. f.*, idea
il, *m., s., def. art.*, the
impiegato, *n. m.*, employee
in, *prep.*, in
indica, *3d s. pres. ind.*, **indicare**,
  to indicate

infatti, *adv.*, in fact
inglese, *adj., pron.*, English
imponente, *adj.*, imposing
insalata, *n. f.*, salad
insomma, *adv.*, in short, then
interessante, *adj.*, interesting
internazionale, *adj.*, international
invece di, *prep.*, instead of
invitato, *adj.*, invited
io, *pers. pron.*, I
Italiani, *n. m., pl.*, Italians

L

latte, *n. m.*, milk
lattuga, *n. f.*, lettuce
lavarsi, *refl. vb.*, to wash oneself
legge, *n. f.*, law
letto, *n. m.*, bed
lezione, *n. f.*, lesson
linea, *n. f.*, line
lista, *n. f.*, menu
litro, *n. m.*, liter
lo, *pron.*, it
località, *n. f.*, place
loro, *rel. pron.*, them, to them

M

ma, *conj.*, but
macedonia di frutta, *n. m.*,
  fruit salad

macchina, *n. f.*, auto, car
maggiorana, *n. f.*, marjoram
magnifico, *adj.*, magnificent
mancia, *n. f.*, tip
mandare, *vb.*, to send
Maria, *n. f.*, Mary
marsala, *n. f.*, Marsala wine
martira, *n. f.*, martyr
medicina, *n. f.*, medicine
medico, *n. m.*, doctor
medioevale, *adj.*, medieval
mezzo, *adj.*, half
mezzogiorno, *n. m.*, noon
mia, *pron.*, my
mila, *pron.*, thousand
Milano, *n. m.*, Milan
mille, *adj.*, thousand; — grazie, many thanks
minuto, *n. m.*, minute
misto, *adj.*, mixed
moglie, *n. f.*, wife
monarca, *n. m.*, monarch
mondo, *n. m.*, world
monumento, *n. m.*, monument
mostrare, *vb.*, to show

N

nati, *pl.*, born
nè, *conj.*, nor
nè ... nè, *conj.*, neither ... nor
negli, *prep. + art., pl.*, in the
negozio, *n. m.*, shop

nella, *prep. + art., s.*, in the
niente, *adv., adj.*, nothing
niente di più, *pron.*, nothing else
no, *adv.*, no
noi, *pers. pron.*, we
noleggio, *n. m.*, rental
nome, *n. m.*, name
non, *adv.*, not
non ... mai, *adv.*, never
nono, *adj.*, ninth
nostro, *adj.*, our
nove, *adj.*, nine; alle —, at nine o'clock
nulla, *adv.*, nothing
numero, *n. m.*, number
Nuova York, *n. f.*, New York
nuovo, *adj.*, new; di —; again

O

o, *conj.*, or
offre, *3d sing., pres. ind.*, offrire, to offer
oggi, *adv.*, today
ogni, *adj.*, each, every
ondulazione, *n. f.*, wave; — permanente, permanent
onnibus, *n. m.*, bus
opera, *n. f.*, opera
ora, *n. f.*, hour; *adv.*, now
ora ora, *adv.*, right away
osteria, *n. f.*, tavern
ottantacinque, *adj.*, eighty-five

P

paga, *3d s., pres. ind.,* **pagare,** to pay; **pagano,** *3d pl., pres. ind.*

pagare, *vb.,* to pay

pagheremo, *1st pl., fut.,* **pagare**

palla, *n. f.,* ball

pane, *n. m.,* bread; — e coperto, cover (restaurant)

panna, *n. f.,* cream

parente, -i, *n. m.,* relative, -s

pare, *3d s., pres. ind.,* **parere,** to seem; **ti pare,** it seems to you

parere, *vb.,* to seem; *n. m.,* opinion

Parigi, *n. f.,* Paris

parla, *3d s., pres. ind.,* **parlare,** to speak; **parlate,** *2d pl., pres.ind.*

parmigiano, *n.m.,* parmesan (cheese)

parte, a-, *adv.,* apart

partenza, *n. f.,* departure

passare, *vb.,* to pass, spend

passaporto, *n. m.,* passport

pasta, *n. f.,* pasta; spaghetti, etc.

pasta dentifricia, *n. f.,* toothpaste

patente, *n. f.,* license

paura, *n. f.,* fear

peccato, *n. m.,* sin, pity, shame

pensare, *vb.,* to think

per, *prep.,* for, to, in order to

perchè, *conj.,* why, because, *so that* (in order that)

perciò, *conj.,* therefore

permettete, *2d pl., pres ind.,* **permettere,** to permit

pesca, -che, *n. f.,* peach, -es

Petrarca, *n. m.,* Petrarch

piace, *3d s., pres. ind.,* **piacere,** to like

piacere, *n. m.,* pleasure

piatto, *n. m,* plate, dish

piccolo, *adj.,* small, short

piedi, a, *n. m.,* on foot

pietanza, *n. f.,* dish, delicacy

pittura, *n. f.,* painting

più, *adj.,* more; **il più,** the most

poco, *adj.,* little, somewhat

poi, *adv.,* then

pomodoro, *n. m.,* tomato

porge, *3d s., pres. ind.,* **porgere,** to hand, give

possiamo, *1st pl., pres. ind.,* **potere,** to be able to

posso, *1st s., pres. ind.,* **potere,** to be able to

potete, *2nd pl., pres. ind.,* **potere,** to be able to

preferisco, *1st s. pres. ind.* **preferire,** to prefer

prendere, *vb.,* to get, to take

prenotare, *vb.,* to reserve; **prenotato,** *p.part.*

prepara, *3d s., pres. ind.,* **preparare** to prepare; **si** —, it is prepared

presentare, *vb.,* to present

prezzemolo, *n. m.,* parsley

prezzo, *n. m.,* price

prima, *n. f.*, first; *adv.*, at first
prima di, *prep.*, before (time)
professore, *n. m.*, professor
pronto, *adj.*, ready
prosciutto, *n. m.*, cured ham
provare, *vb.*, to try on; provato,
    p. part.
può, *3d s. pres. ind.*, potere, to
    be able to
qua, *adv.*, here

Q

qualche, *adj.*, some
quale, *pron.*, which
quasi, *adv.*, almost
qualsiasi, *adj.*, any
quando, *conj.*, when
quanto, *pron.*, much (how)
quattordicesimo, *adj.*, fourteenth
quelli, *m., pl., pron.*, those who;
    the ones who
questo -a, *m., f., s., pron., adj.*,
    this, this one
quinto, *adj.*, fifth

R

raccomanda, *3d s., pres. ind.*,
    raccomandare, to recommend
re, *n. m.*, king
ricetta, *n. f.*, recipe
Rinascimento, *n. m.*, Renaissance

rinomato, *adj.*, renowned
rinovare, *vb.*, renew
riposarsi,*vb.*, to rest; si sono
    riposati, they rested
ristorante, *n. m.*, restaurant
ritornando, *pres. part.*,
    ritornare, to return
ritorneranno, *3d pl., fut.*,
    ritornare, to return
rosso, *adj.*, red

S

sa, *3d s., pres. ind.*, sapere, to
    know; sai, *2nd s., pres. ind.*
sala da pranzo, *n. f.*, dining room
sala di bellezza, *n. f.*, beauty parlor
salsa, *n. f.*, sauce
santa, *n. f.*, saint
saporito,-a, *adj.*, tasty
saprà, *3d s., fut.*, sapere, to
    know. Mi saprà dire, can you
    tell me?
scarpa, *n. f.*, shoe
scherzi, *2nd s., pres. ind.*,
    scherzare, to joke
scherzo, -i, *n. m.*, joke, -s
sciacquare, *vb.*, to rinse
scienza, *n. f.*, science
scusate, *2nd pl., imp.*, scusare, to
    excuse; scusatemi, excuse me.
scusi, *2nd s. imp.*, scusare, to
    excuse
se, *conj.*, if, whether

secolo, *n. m.*, century

sedono, *3d pl., pres. ind.*, sedere, to sit

seduto, *adj.*, seated

sei, *2nd s., pres. ind.*, essere, to be

sempre, *adv.*, always

senatore, *n. m.*, senator

senti, *2nd imp.*, sentire, to listen, look; sentite, *2nd pl.*

senza, *prep.*, without

sessanta, *adj.*, sixty

settimana, *n. f.*, week

si, *pron.*, himself, herself, themselves (m., f.)

sì, *adv.*, yes

siamo *1st pl., pres. ind.*, essere, to be; — stati, we have been

siccome, *conj.*, as (since)

Siciliani, *n. m.*, Sicilians

siete, *2nd pl., pres. ind.*, essere, to be

signore, *n. m.*, sir, mister, si —, *n. m.*, yes sir

sincerità, *n. f.*, sincerity

sinistra, *pron.*, left side

so, *1st s., pres. ind.*, sapere, to know

sofà, *n. m.*, sofa

solo, *m., adj., pron.*, alone

sono, *1st s., pres. ind.*, essere, to be

speciale, *adj.*, special

specializza, *3d s., pres. ind.*, specializzare, to specialize

Spagna, *n. f.*, Spain

spettacolo, -i, *n. m.*, spectacle, -s

spiegare, *vb.*, to explain

sposa, *n. f.*, wife

spremuta, *n. f.*, squeezed juice

sta, *3d s., pres.ind.*, stare, to be, to fit

stabilito, *adj.*, established

stamattina, *n. f.*, this morning

stampa *3d s., pres. ind.*, stampare, to stamp

stanchi, *adj., pl.*, tired

stanza, *n. f.*, room; — da bagno, *n. f.*, bathroom

stare, *vb.*, to stay, be, look

stasera, *adv.*, tonight

strano, *adj.*, strange

Stati Uniti, *n. m., pl.*, United States

statua, *n. f.*, statue

stiamo, *1st pl., pres. ind.*, stare, to be; stiamo faccendo, we are doing

storico, *adj.*, historic

studente, *n. m.*, student

stupendo, *adj.*, marvelous

su, *prep.*, on

T

tanto, *adv.*, so much

tassa, *n. f.*, tax, toll

tassì, *n. m.*, taxi

tassista, *n. m.*, taxi driver

tardi, più, *adv.*, later

tavola, *n. f.*, table

teatro, *n. m.*, theater

telefono, *n. m.*, telephone

telegramma, *n. m.*, telegram
tempo, *n. m.*, weather
teologia, *n. f.*, theology
terminato, *adj.*, finished
terra, *n. f.*, earth
tesoro, *n. m.*, treasure
testa, *n. f.*, head
ti, *pron.*, yourself, to you
toga, *n. f.*, toga
tornare, to turn, return;
    tornano, *3d pl., pres. ind.*
tra, *prep.*, within
trasportato, *adj.*, transported
trattoria, *n. m.*, restaurant
tre, *adj.*, three
trentina, *n. f.*, about thirty
trionfo, *n. m.*, triumph
trippa, *n. f.*, tripe
tritato, *adj.*, ground, chopped
troppo, *adj.*, too much, too
trovare, *vb.*, to find
tu, *2nd s., pron.*, you
tubetto, *n. m.*, tube
turista, -i, *n. m.*, tourist, -s
tuttavia, *conj.*, however
tutti, *pron.*, everyone
tutti e due, *pron.*, both of us,
    you, them
tutto, *adj., pron.*, all

U

ufficiale, *n. m.*, officer
ultimo, *pron.*, last

undicesimo, *adj.*, eleventh
università, *n. f.*, university
uno, -a, *indef. art., pron.*, one
uomini, *n. m., pl.*, men
uscite, *2nd pl., pres. ind.*, uscire,
    to leave

V

vale, *3d s., pres. ind.*, valere, to
    be worth
valigia, *n. f.*, suitcase
vedere, *vb.*, to see; vedo, *1st s.*,
    pres. ind.
venire, *vb.*, to come; venite, *2nd*
    pl., pres. ind.
vero, *adj.*, true, real
verso, *prep.*, toward
veste, *n. f.*, dress
vesti, *2nd s., pres. ind.*, vestirsi,
    to dress oneself
vestiario, *n. m.*, clothing
vi, *pron.*, you, to you, for you,
    yourselves
via, *n. f.*, road, way
viaggio, *n. m.*, trip
vicino (là), *adv.*, near
vicino, *prep.*, near
vino, *n. m.*, wine
virtù, *n. f.*, virtue
visitare, *vb.*, to visit; visitato,
    p. part.
visiteremo, *1st pl., fut.*, visitare,
    to visit

vista, *n. f.,* view
voglio, *1st s., pres. ind.,* volere,
    to want; vogliamo, *1st pl.,*
    pres. ind.
voi, *2nd pl., pers. pron.,* you
vorrei, *1st s., cond.,* volere, to
    want; vuoi, *2nd s. pres. ind.,*
    vuole, *3d s.;* vuole dire,
    verbal phr., that means

Also written by Dr. Joseph Privitera . . .

A Treasury of Italian Cuisine
Recipes, Sayings and Proverbs in Italian and English
Illustrated by Sharon Privitera

Don Peppino (a.k.a Joseph) Privitera outlines the basics of hearty and delicious Italian cooking in this appealing bilingual cookbook. Among the 60 recipes in Italian and English are such staples as *Cozze alla Parmigiana* (Baked Mussels), *Minestrone, Salsa di Pomodoro* (Basic Tomato Sauce), *Ossobuco al Marsala* (Veal Shanks in Marsala), and *Cannoli Siciliani* (Sicilian Cannoli), all adapted for the modern cook and the North American kitchen. Chapters include: Antipasti, Soups, Pasta and Sauces, Meat, Fish and Fowl, Side Dishes, Salads, and Fruits and Desserts. Line drawings, proverbs and bits of folk wisdom add to the volume's charm. This book is the perfect gift for students of the Italian culinary tradition, culture and language.
146 pages • 5 x 7 • line drawings • ISBN 0-7818-0740-9
• $11.95hc • W • (149)

Beginner's Sicilian
Learn Sicilian vocabulary, grammar, and useful phrases in ten concise, practical lessons. Here is basic language instruction with a whole new perspective, designed to meet the bilingual needs of the traveling businessperson, tourist and student.
159 pages • 5½ x 8½ • ISBN 0-7818-0640-2
• $11.95pb • W • (716)

OTHER ITALIAN TITLES FROM HIPPOCRENE BOOKS . . .

Italian-English/English-Italian Practical Dictionary
Large Print Edition
35,000 entries • 433 pages • 5¼ x 8½ • ISBN 0-7818-0354-3
• $12.95pb • (201)

Italian Handy Dictionary
3,000 entries • 120 pages • 5 x 7¾ • ISBN 0-7818-0011.-0
• $8.95pb • (196)

Hippocrene Children's Illustrated Italian Dictionary
English-Italian/Italian-English
500 entries • 94 pages • 8½ x 11 • ISBN 0-7818-0771-9
• $14.95hc • (355)

Italian-English/English-Italian Dictionary and Phrasebook
2,500 entries • 213 pages • 3¾ x 7 • ISBN 0-7818-0812-X
• $11.95pb • (137)

Mastering Italian
341 pages • 5½ x 8½ • ISBN 0-87052-057-1 • $11.95pb • (517)
2 cassettes: ISBN 0-7818-0333-0 • $12.95 • (521)

Mastering Advanced Italian
278 pages • 5½ x 8½ • ISBN 0-7818-0333-0 • $14.95pb • (160)
2 cassettes: ISBN 0-7818-0334-9 • $12.95 • (161)

Dictionary of 1,000 Italian Proverbs
131 pages • 5½ x 8½ • ISBN 0-7818-0458-2 • $11.95pb • (370)

Treasury of Italian Love
127 pages • 5¼ x 7¼ • ISBN 0-7818-0352-7 • $11.95hc • (587)
2 cassettes: ISBN 0-7818-0366-7 • $12.95hc • (581)

HIPPOCRENE BEGINNER'S SERIES

Arabic For Beginners, *Revised Edition*
240 pages • 5½ x 8¼ • ISBN 0-7818-0841-3 • NA • $11.95pb • (229)

Beginner's Albanian
150 pages • 5 x 7 • ISBN 0-7818-0816-2 • W • $14.95pb • (537)

Beginner's Armenian
209 pages • 5½ x 8½ • ISBN 0-7818-0723-9 • W • $14.95pb • (226)

Beginner's Assyrian
138 pages • 5½ x 8½ • ISBN 0-7818-0677-1 • W • $11.95pb • (763)

Beginner's Bulgarian
207 pages • 5½ x 8½ • ISBN 0-7818-0300-4 • W • $9.95pb • (76)

Beginner's Chinese
150 pages • 5½ x 8½ • ISBN 0-7818-0566-X • W • $14.95pb • (690)

Beginner's Czech
167 pages • 5½ x 8½ • ISBN 0-7818-0231-8 • W • $9.95pb • (74)

Beginner's Dutch
173 pages • 5½ x 8½ • ISBN 0-7818-0735-2 • W • $14.95pb • (248)

Beginner's Esperanto
342 pages • 5½ x 8½ • ISBN 0-7818-0230-X • W • $14.95pb • (51)

Beginner's Gaelic
224 pages • 5½ x 8½ • ISBN 0-7818-0726-3 • W • $14.95pb • (255)

Beginner's Hungarian
101 pages • 5½ x 7 • ISBN 0-7818-0209-1 • W • $7.95pb • (68)

Beginner's Irish
150 pages • 5 x 7 • ISBN 0-7818-0784-0 • W • $14.95pb • (320)

Beginner's Japanese
290 pages • 6 x 8 • ISBN 0-7818-0234-2 • W • $11.95pb • (53)

Beginner's Lithuanian
471 pages • 6 x 9 • ISBN 0-7818-0678-X • W • $19.95pb • (764)

Beginner's Maori
121 pages • 5½ x 8½ • ISBN 0-7818-0605-4 • NA • $8.95pb • (703)

Beginner's Persian
288 pages • 5½ x 8½ • ISBN 0-7818-0567-8 • NA • $14.95pb • (696)

Beginner's Polish
118 pages • 5½ x 8½ • ISBN 0-7818-0299-7 • W • $9.95pb • (82)

Beginner's Romanian
105 pages • 5½ x 8½ • ISBN 0-7818-0208-3 • W • $7.95pb • (79)

Beginner's Russian
131 pages • 5½ x 8½ • ISBN 0-7818-0232-6 • W • $9.95pb • (61)

Beginner's Sicilian
159 pages • 5½ x 8½ • ISBN 0-7818-0640-2 • W • $11.95pb • (716)

Beginner's Swahili
200 pages • 5½ x 8½ • ISBN 0-7818-0335-7 • W • $9.95pb • (52)

Beginner's Turkish
300 pages • 5 x 7½ • ISBN 0-7818-0679-8 • NA • $14.95pb • (765)

Beginner's Ukrainian
130 pages • 5½ x 8½ • ISBN 0-7818-0443-4 • W • $11.95pb • (88)

Beginner's Vietnamese
515 pages • 7 x 10 • ISBN 0-7818-0411-6 • $19.95pb • W • (253)

Beginner's Welsh
171 pages • 5½ x 8½ • ISBN 0-7818-0589-9 • W • $9.95pb • (712)

Prices subject to change without prior notice.
To order **Hippocrene Books**, contact your local bookstore, call (718) 454-2366, or write to: Hippocrene Books, 171 Madison Avenue, New York, NY 10016. Please enclose check or money order adding $5.00 shipping (UPS) for the first book and $.50 for each additional title.